DEMOS

Demos is an independent think tank committed to radical thinking on the long-term problems facing the UK and other advanced industrial societies.

It aims to develop ideas – both theoretical and practical – to help shape the politics of the twenty first century, and to improve the breadth and quality of political debate.

Demos publishes books and a regular journal and undertakes substantial empirical and policy oriented research projects. Demos is a registered charity.

In all its work Demos brings together people from a wide range of backgrounds in business, academia, government, the voluntary sector and the media to share and cross-fertilise ideas and experiences.

For further information and
subscription details please contact:
Demos
Panton House
25 Haymarket
London SW1Y 4EN
Telephone: 0171 321 2200
Facsimile: 0171 321 2342
email: mail@demos.co.uk
www.demos.co.uk

Other publications available from Demos:

The Common Sense of Community
The Creative City
The Freedom of the City
The Return of the Local
The Wealth and Poverty of Networks

Living together

Community life on mixed tenure estates

Ben Jupp

with additional research by
James Sainsbury and Oliver Akers-Douglas

First published in 1999 by
Demos
Panton House
25 Haymarket
London SW1Y 4EN
Telephone: 0171 321 2200
Facsimile: 0171 321 2342
email: mail@demos.co.uk

ISBN 1 898309 15 9
Printed in Great Britain by Redwood Books, Trowbridge
Design by Lindsay Nash

Contents

Acknowledgements

This report is the output of a year-long research project to which many people contributed. I am very grateful to the Housing Corporation and National House-Building Council (NHBC) who provided the funding which made the research possible. In particular, Adrian Moran and Chris Watts from the Housing Corporation and Imtiaz Farookhi, Derek Hamilton-Knight and Sarah Hamilton from the NHBC not only helped support the project but provided useful suggestions about how to focus the research and feedback on the report.

Studying communities on new housing estates in Britain is not always glamorous research. It is clear why anthropologists traditionally chose to study communities on Pacific Islands and other warm environments. Four researchers at Demos – James Sainsbury, Oliver Akers-Douglas, Tim Lewin and JJ Jaxson – spent much time visiting recommended estates, sometimes only to find the estate half built, and tramping often wet and cold streets. They also tracked down most of the literature and interviewed many of the experts. I have greatly appreciated their help. Much of the survey fieldwork was also undertaken by Public Attitude Surveys (PAS) and NOP. We are grateful to Mark Peters and Sandra Jowett of PAS and Rose Neville of NOP for their input and efficient production of the results.

The research also benefited from considerable advice from a number of housing professionals, academics and policy analysts. In particular, I would like to thank the advisory group: Ian Cole and Sigrid Shayer of Sheffield Hallam University, Keith Colley of Metropolitan Home Ownership, Kathleen Dunmore of the House Builders Federation, Liz Greenhalgh of Comedia, Hugo Hinsley of the Architectural Association, Keith Kintrea of the University of Glasgow, David Page, independent housing researcher and consultant, John Perry of the Charted Institute of Housing and Marilyn Taylor of the University of Brighton. We also benefited from the interest shown in the project by the Joseph Rowntree Foundation, the London Planning Advisory Group and National Housing Federation. Many of the people who we interviewed on the estates did so on the basis that their contribution was anonymous. Their help and time was greatly appreciated.

Finally, colleagues at Demos have helped draw out the ideas, advise on the research and manage the project, and have published this report. I am particularly indebted to Tom Bentley, Perri 6, Ian Christie, Richard Warner, Lindsay Nash, Debbie Porter, Tom Hampson and Jean-Nicholas Fiévet who all made important contributions.

Ben Jupp, September 1999

Executive summary

1. The creation of mixed communities – areas with an economically diverse population – is an aspiration for much current planning, housing and regeneration policy. Neighbourhoods with a mix of rich and poor residents are described by politicians through a host positive adjectives: 'vibrant', 'balanced' and 'inclusive'.

2. Yet beneath the surface of warm community rhetoric, policy-makers are struggling to resolve a very serious debate over the pros and cons of building private and subsidised housing next to each other. Advocates argue that mixed communities sustain better local economies and public services, such as schools, than do uniformly poor areas. They also suggest that mixed communities have social advantages: residents in work can help those without work access the labour market; successful residents can be role models; a more united and inclusive society develops.

3. In contrast, critics fear that mixed communities are likely to be divided. They worry that tensions develop between the better off who own their homes and the poorer families in council or housing association properties. They argue that the better off want to live apart and that ensuring new developments contain a mix of tenures is an unsustainable form of social engineering.

4. The Government's desire to develop new planning and housing policies makes the resolution of these debates all the more urgent. But that is hampered by a lack of evidence about commu-

nity life on mixed estates. Too many arguments are fed by anecdote and speculation.

5. This report helps to provide the evidence. It draws on interviews with over 1,000 residents of ten mixed tenure estates. In particular it considers the networks of support and points of tension which develop in those communities.

Key findings

6. **Most residents are not particularly worried nor inspired by the mixed nature of their estates.** Only about a quarter of respondents perceived any problems and a quarter any benefits arising from mix. The rest are agnostic. Where problems are perceived they usually tend to exert a minor influence on people's overall perception: **no significant correlation existed between residents' overall feelings about the estate and their perceptions of whether mix causes problems or not.** Conversely, when benefits are perceived they are often vague, such as a general belief that it is good for people from all backgrounds to live together. Only about one in ten respondents mentioned specific benefits, such as creating a good physical environment or attracting shops.

7. **Street level mixing is preferable to separating tenures in different zones on an estate.** Although some residents felt that owners would rather live apart from tenants, residents of mixed streets did not perceive more problems with mixing than those of zoned estates. They were also significantly more positive about the estates overall. Given that street level mixing helps reduce the chance that certain streets of exclusively social housing will be develop a bad image, integration has advantages over separating tenures into different blocks.

8. **Like non-mixed estates, mixed estates do occasionally run into specific problems** associated with vandalism, noise, children on the streets and the like. Sometimes tenants are blamed in general. In those circumstances a couple of our estates developed broader social

tensions. The mix does not cause the problems, but very occasionally it can help polarise communities which in turn leads to further problems. This reinforces the need to prevent or rectify problems in the first place, and to break down stereotypes of residents of different tenures.

9. **Most relatively new mixed estates are not characterised by inclusive social networks.** Social policy analysts should therefore be very careful about making claims for a new sort of community on mixed estates. Only two-fifths of our respondents knew any residents with a different tenure. Only one-fifth could ask for help or advice from a resident with a different tenure. The hope that the current models of mixed tenure estates will foster widespread mutual support between people from different economic groups, considerably broaden understanding between groups and or introduce role models into an area appears largely misplaced.

10. **Social contact between residents increases gradually over time, but the formation of mixed communities often remains constrained by the physical separation of tenures.** On those estates in which private and social housing is confined to different streets, only one in five respondents knew the name of a single resident with a different tenure. The findings suggest that, even after many years, most residents of such estates will not belong to an inclusive community because most people only get to know their near neighbours. **The street is a much stronger social unit than the estate.** On estates with higher amounts of street level integration, nearly half knew someone with a different tenure. On many streets, contact was considerably higher.

11. **Fostering greater estate-wide contact is likely to be an uphill struggle.** Most British do not think that they share many common interests with their neighbours. Local amenities such as shops and pubs are rarely used for meeting new people. Only 15 per cent of respondents had got to know any fellow residents at the local shops and 7 per cent at the local pub despite the widespread use of such facilities. **Schools are by far the most important non-street site for local contact.**

Even then, one-third of parents had not got to know any other estate residents through their child's school. The best hope for fostering estate-wide communities is to increase the length of time people live on the estate (which may have other drawbacks such as requiring people to commute further) or to develop better local mechanisms for sharing information and resources, for example through local web pages and newsletters, so that people are aware of their common interests. Community centres can also make a significant difference, but they tend to be used by only a small minority.

12. The lack of close estate-wide community on many new estates (mixed or not) may make it harder for people to come together to tackle common problems, but by no means impossible. Many people are used to working with others who they do not know very well. **Given the right structures and some sense of local belonging, residents can get together to tackle common problems such as poor maintenance or rising crime.** Those structures may be, for example, a small neighbourhood group or individual who acts as focal point for others if serious problems develop. Supporting these often dormant structures and individuals is often as important as trying to constantly get a large proportion of residents involved in community groups. Local workers also need to quickly identify which issues have the potential to galvanise people into action so that ad hoc groups can be facilitated.

13. **The policy agenda for mixed tenure estates is to develop the positive features of community – trust, common standards of public behaviour and collective action – while recognising that most people's social networks lie beyond the estate.** That task will best be achieved neither by relying solely on fostering informal community structures nor by extending the role of the existing statutory agencies. Instead, the potential lies with people and institutions who straddle the informal–official divide. Community workers, wardens, senior caretakers and community police who are rooted in local conditions but also bring some external authority are examples of that principle. They help facilitate common living in areas in which residents

tend to know only a few others. A major public policy challenge is to develop more such roles. In our crowded island we need people who perform them in many neighbourhoods, mixed or otherwise.

1. Introduction

Relationships between neighbours have long provided the source of some of our most popular entertainment – from local gossip to the story lines of soap operas. Over the last century, investigating community relations has also become a legitimate academic activity. Anthropology – the discipline whose hallmark has been the study of local societies – has grown so large that just one American association of anthropologists now boasts over 10,000 members.[1] But social relations between local residents also generate more than passing interest among politicians, policy analysts, planners, housing professionals, police, and a host of other public service workers.

Not only can disputes and tensions between residents lower their quality of life, they can have a negative effect on a whole area. Politicians and other policy-makers fear that divided communities are less likely to come together to tackle common challenges such as crime or improving the environment. Neighbourhood disputes also make it harder to manage estates. And as demand for housing has fallen in some areas, landlords and local authorities are concerned that friction can prompt residents to leave and deter new people from moving in.

Conversely, good relations between neighbours have traditionally been perceived to be important sources of support for individuals and neighbourhoods. In particular, local residents are increasingly being asked by politicians and public agencies to come together as a community to support schools and other local services.[2] Sometimes neighbourhoods are also perceived to be important places for mutual support, such as sharing the burden of looking after children.[3] Communitarians such professor Amitai Etzioni, the influential

American sociologist, argue that strong local communities also help engender a sense of responsibility: 'interpersonal bonds encourage members to abide by shared values such as "do not throw trash out of your window".'[4]

It is no surprise therefore that in designing and managing housing estates, planners, developers and housing managers have often sought to encourage good social relations. For example, more and more local authorities run neighbourhood dispute arbitration services. And community development activities such as the formation of residents groups on estates is gaining an increasingly high political profile.

One type of local society is currently attracting particular attention from policy-makers and politicians: those which develop on estates containing both richer and poorer households. These 'mixed communities' are being encouraged by building private housing and subsidised council or housing association properties on the same estates. For example, the Urban Task Force recently strongly endorsed mixing tenures on new developments and re-developments of old estates. Often such neighbourhoods are described as having a better sort of community. However, little consensus or evidence has yet emerged about the patterns of social relations which emerge on these estates and what particular opportunities or challenges they present for local residents and public service professionals.

Some policy-makers believe that mixed tenure estates can help foster contact between people with different economic circumstances in a way which is economically and culturally beneficial to individuals and society at large. They suggest that by bringing together people from different walks of life, mixed housing developments can help foster a more inclusive society. Some hope that richer and poorer families will create a synergy of resources in an area, between those who have money but little time and others who have time but little money, for example. The social and cultural characteristics of mixed estates are often compared favourably to those of large council estates, which are seen as communities detached from the labour market and sometimes lacking good role models.

However, some housing managers and some developers fear that, rather than creating a more inclusive society, combining tenures actually leads to disputes and tension between owners and tenants. They worry that owners and tenants may have different priorities or different attitudes towards an area. They are concerned that owners, in particular, want to live apart from more needy sections of the population and that forcing people to live together requires unacceptable costs in terms of incentives or impositions upon liberty.

This report considers the extent to which these hopes and fears for local societies on mixed tenure estates are borne out by experience. It draws on new research into community life on ten mixed tenure estates. When combined with analysis of the impact of mixing on local economies, public services and image, the research should help policy-makers better decide when mixed tenure developments are appropriate and how to improve community relations on such estates.

- Chapter two outlines why political interest has grown in mixed estates.
- Chapter three considers the key policy questions about local social and cultural conditions on mixed tenure estates and the extent to which previous research illuminates these issues.
- Chapter four presents new evidence about patterns of social contact and mutual support between residents on mixed tenure estates.
- Chapter five presents new evidence about residents' feelings about living on mixed tenure estates and the extent to which tensions and disputes develop.
- Chapter six concludes by considering lessons for the development of new mixed tenure estates and for fostering positive attributes of community life within mixed neighbourhoods.

2. The rise of interest in mixed tenure developments

> 'We all know the problems of our poorest neighbourhoods – decaying housing, unemployment, street crime and drugs. People who can, move out. Nightmare neighbours move in. Shops, banks and other vital services close.... Over the last two decades the gap between these 'worst estates' and the rest of the country has grown. It has left us with a situation that no civilised society should tolerate.[5] *Tony Blair*

Many of the roots of modern social policy lie in nineteenth century attempts to alleviate the problems of poor health, housing and education which characterised the slums of industrial cities. In the decades since, the problems of the poorest neighbourhoods have periodically resurfaced into public policy debate. New housing for inner city residents was one of the great post-war government projects. Margaret Thatcher famously noted that the government needed to do something about the plight of inner cities on winning the 1987 election.

Today, the plight of the worst neighbourhoods is back on the political map. Living in a neighbourhood with bad housing, few job prospects, a failing school, fear of crime, lack of transport and a negative image is often portrayed by politicians and the media as the epitome of social exclusion – the loss of access to the most important life chances that a modern society offers.[6] For some politicians, and those working for local and national government, the voluntary sector and increasing numbers of private firms, tackling the social, economic and environmental decline of certain neighbourhoods has become one of the most pressing challenges for the start of the new century. In this chapter we consider why this concern has arisen and one way in which the government hopes that such problems will not become concentrated in particular neighbourhoods in the future – by ensuring that new developments contain a mix of private and subsidised accommodation.

Mounting concern about the segregation of rich and poor

One of the unenviable reputations already gained by the last two decades of the twentieth century is that of a period of winners and losers. The most frequently quoted, and probably most revealing, indicator of increasing inequality is displayed by the way average incomes among different economic groups have changed. Between 1979 and 1995 the incomes of the richest tenth of the population grew by over 60 per cent. In contrast, the incomes of the poorest tenth rose by only 10 per cent (before housing costs) or fell by 8 per cent (after housing costs). That represented a considerable change from the 1960s and 1970s during which time the incomes of the poorest rose fastest.[7]

Many people also appear as trapped in poverty as they have always been. Of course, not everyone who is poor in one year is poor in the next year: many people's relative position changes for the better or worse each year. A few make spectacular rises from poverty to wealth, and vice versa. But the high profile rags to riches stories of some of Britain's most successful entrepreneurs are completely at odds with most people's experience. When people get richer or poorer they tend to do so only marginally, and frequently return to their former position within a few years. Compared to twenty years ago the likelihood of people moving from being relatively poor to being relatively better off appears to have slightly declined.[8] They are as constrained by poor education, unemployment, ill health and old age as ever before.

Reaction against that rising individual inequality has been relatively muted in comparison to the political concern which such conditions provoked during the immediate post-war decades. The only Labour government of the period has not increased the level of most people's basic safety net in real terms.

There is, however, one aspect of Britain's diverging economic conditions which has caught public and political attention: the way in which some areas have greatly declined while others have boomed. In the

1980s, concern arose primarily around broad regional differences – economic growth in the South and contraction in the North – and around the prospects for inner cities. In the 1990s the focus has shifted towards the neighbourhood level. Much Government policy is directed at small areas: regenerating the worst estates, education action zones, employment action zones, health action zones and a host of other initiatives.

The concentration of problems in small areas is borne out by economic and social indicators. Between the censuses of 1981 and 1991 the greatest divergence in prosperity and quality of life indicators occurred at the level of wards. Studies suggest that the gap between affluent and poor wards continued during the 1990s. As the Government's Social Exclusion Unit recently highlighted, the poorest five per cent of wards have more than twice the national level of unemployment and almost three times the number of children in low earning households.[9]

In particular, local authority housing estates have suffered. Some are reasonable. But a rising proportion suffer economic, social and environmental problems. One recent study of twenty unpopular council estates found that by 1991 unemployment among their residents was three times the national average. They concluded that 'the fear of social breakdown resulting from the increasing concentration of needy and vulnerable households was so acute that special localised measures to reinforce community stability were constantly needed.'[10]

The problems of the worst estates

Why do many estates have particularly high levels of social and economic deprivation?

One answer is simple: because residents have lost their jobs. For example, since 1981 Britain's twenty major cities have lost over 500,000 jobs. In particular, neighbourhoods which were focused around a single factory or mine have been disproportionately affected by the economic shift away from such industries.

Another simple answer is even more important: a lot of particularly needy people have been moved into social housing estates. Over the past twenty years, council and housing association tenants have been drawn from an increasingly deprived section of the population, as government spending on social housing has dropped and resources concentrated on the most needy. In 1972, 130,000 new homes were built by local authorities and housing associations. In 1997, just 29,000 were built.[11] With such scarce supply, only those in desperate circumstances tend to be given houses. For example, only about a fifth of lettings by housing associations are now given to those in full-time work. According to one source, half of new tenants now have an income of less than £75 a week.[12]

This concentration of the poorest has been compounded by changes in the way in which housing has been subsidised. The subsidy given to councils and housing associations has been reduced, and rents have therefore risen. These rises do not affect those poorest sections of society who are entitled to housing benefit, but reduce the attraction of social housing for those who are not entitled to housing benefit.

As the more affluent have moved out of social housing and the poorest moved in, the economic profile of tenants has diverged more and more from that of the population as a whole. The proportion in full-time work has halved in less than twenty years. By 1993, 45 per cent of social housing tenants were in the poorest 20 per cent of the population.[13] That is in stark contrast to the decades immediately following the Second World War in which council housing was as equally the preserve of the employed as the economically inactive, and when a substantial minority who lived on such estates had incomes above the national average (see Figure 1 over).[14]

In other words, council housing estates simply allow us to clearly see the symptoms of wider social and economic problems in our society because people suffering such problems are bunched together in them.

Many people also believe that a third, more complex answer exists to the question of why residents of some housing estates have particularly high levels of deprivation – that living on some estates actually causes problems. In other words, the neediness of residents comes not just from the lack of local jobs or the needs they brought with them, but the environment in which they are forced to live.

The nature of the problems caused by living on a council estate

The idea that living in some neighbourhoods actually creates problems for residents is not new. Traditionally, the poor have often been forced

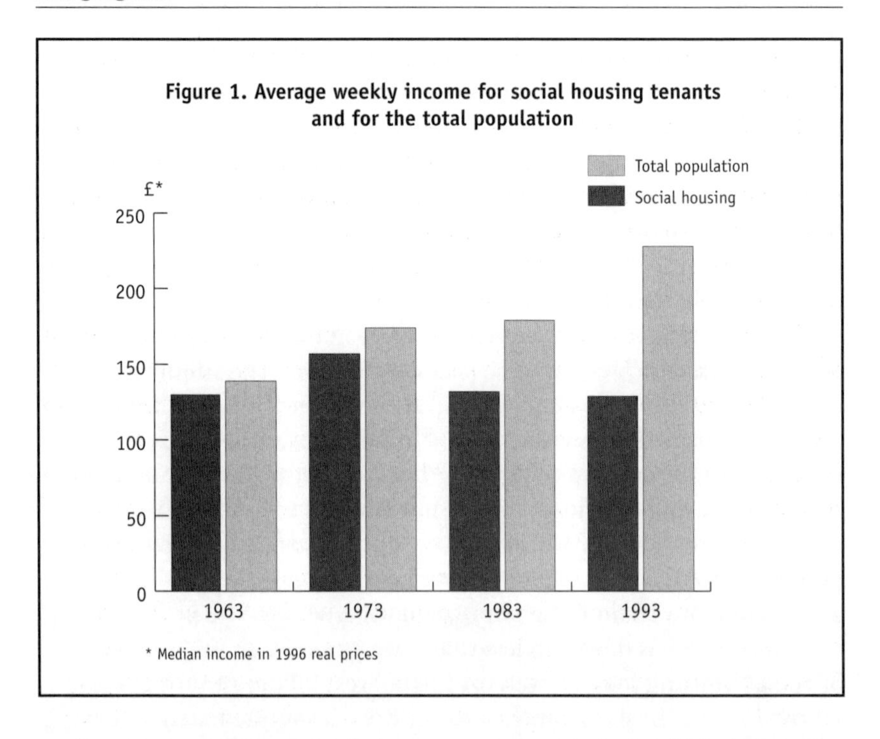

Figure 1. Average weekly income for social housing tenants and for the total population

to live in conditions which have exacerbated their difficulties. For example, the historically poor environmental conditions of many poor neighbourhoods – with the presence of polluting factories and lack of good sanitation – undoubtedly contributed to the ill health of their residents and hence their further disadvantage.

Today, those environmental disadvantages have usually been reduced. But some policy experts suggest that residents of poor neighbourhoods are still handicapped by one or more of four factors.

1. Little money circulates in the local economy

Because residents have little money they are unable to support a range of local shops and amenities. Consequently, they suffer inconvenience and higher transport costs in order to receive goods and services. That was one of the main reasons why one working paper of the Commission on Social Justice argued that 'being poor in a poor area is worse than poverty which is more thinly scattered among rich people'.[15]

Few local business can, in turn, lead to fewer local jobs. A spiral of no local market, no local businesses, no local jobs, no local market can develop.

2. The poor image of an area in itself acts as a barrier to employment and other opportunities

Social housing, many believe, has come to be associated with problems and its residents tainted by association. In the words of one recent report, 'too many modern housing developments are stigmatised by single tenure development.'[16] In particular, large estates gain local notoriety. Residents often complain that they are discriminated against by employers and businesses because of where they live.[17]

Some commentators also fear that the databases of businesses formalise that discrimination: that areas are written off on the basis of the characteristics of the majority of residents.[18] They worry that simple classifications of residents in different postcodes mean that companies only bother to invest and market products in wealthy areas.

3. Local public services can not cope with very high numbers of needy residents

Local authorities, health authorities, the police and other public agencies are allocated resources that are partly determined by the neediness of the population they serve. Everyone should, therefore, receive the same service. But it is possible that, even if public services in poorer area receive more financial resources, they may be disadvantaged in other ways. For example, recruiting good GPs is notoriously difficult in poor neighbourhoods. The turnover of teachers is also higher in schools on poor estates, making it harder to maintain a top quality service. Some people also argue that if a very large proportion of pupils come from disadvantaged backgrounds it is extremely difficult to create a successful school.[19]

4. Poor social and cultural conditions

Another, more contentious, view is that concentrations of poverty-stricken households lead to local communities that lack adequate social or cultural resources, thus further disadvantaging those residents.

A popular idea is that uniformly deprived communities with few people in work lack good role models. For example, one study of unpopular estates in Britain cites a resident who noted:

> 'You can hold a can of Special Brew and a spliff and walk around in front of the children without being ashamed – what kind of a role model is that? "Jones" to keep up with do help solve problems, but we haven't got any Jones ... there are so many irresponsible people here.'[20]

Another contention is that communities on deprived housing estates are less linked into the informal labour market because so few members of the community have jobs. Studies do suggest that people often hear about jobs through word of mouth and that the job seekers who mainly socialise with other unemployed people may have fewer of such informal opportunities.[21] That would suggest that living in a community dominated by those without jobs cuts off a potentially important way back into the labour market.

Some commentators also suggest that better-off residents can be more assertive in demanding better services from local authorities, schools, the police, businesses and other organisations, and are therefore potentially important assets to the community.[22]

These four issues – local economy, image, public services and society – can be conceived as contributing to downward spiral in an area: high initial concentrations of need which in turn further disadvantage residents and therefore exacerbate poverty in the neighbourhood. Figure two represents that process in a very simplified form.

Responses to the problems of concentrated areas of poverty

The traditional response to the extra hurdles that residents of poor neighbourhoods face has been to target resources at such areas. Examples of area-specific action litter social policy over the past century and a half. From earliest public health measures in the nineteenth century to slum clearance during the post-war era to the development corporations of the 1980s, certain neighbourhoods have been targeted for improvements to the physical, social and economic environment.

Figure 2. Simple cycle of deprivation

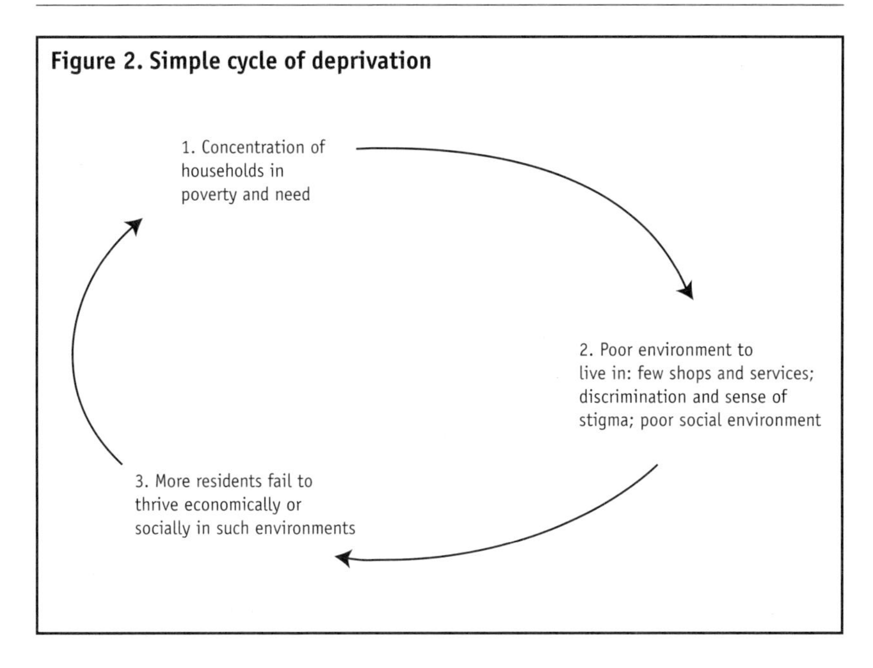

That trend continues today. A raft of new initiatives has been developed over the past few years which aims to improve the conditions in deprived neighbourhoods as a way to boost the life chances of their residents. Many of these have focused on trying to strengthen the social environment rather than the physical environment (often the primary objective of past initiatives), for example with a variety of initiatives to support community groups and reduce crime. The current government has targeted resources through a number of area-based initiatives such as health and education action zones.

But there has also been some questioning of the long-term effectiveness of policies that target resources at the physical, economic and social environment in deprived areas. Many of the houses that have been built to replace poor quality stock have themselves become unpopular. Many of the shops and factory units that have been built on deprived estates have proved hard to let. Despite considerably higher spending per pupil, many schools that serve areas of concentrated deprivation still struggle.

In response, renewed emphasis has also been given to intervening at the start of the cycle of deprivation (point 1 in our diagram). In some people's perception, the concentration of households in poverty is, in itself, such a burden for an estate that almost no amount of amelioration to the environment will compensate for that disadvantage. They suggest that the long-term solution is simply to avoid such concentrations in the first place by using the planning system and other policies to bring richer and poorer households into the same neighbourhoods. Then, so the argument goes, the poor will at least have shops near them, will possibly have jobs working in these shops, will not be discriminated against because of where they live, may have better local public services and both the better and worse off may benefit from being members of communities with a broader range of experience and resources than if they lived apart.

The rise of interest in mixed tenure developments

The emphasis on avoiding areas of concentrated poverty, rather than simply trying to offset disadvantage caused by such concentration, appears to be gaining considerable acceptance by policy-makers. A variety of central and local government documents increasingly emphasises that, where possible, new housing or redeveloped housing estates should not solely comprise of private housing or social (council and housing association) housing. Rather, the different tenures with their different population groups should be brought together.

A few such 'mixed tenure' estates have always been built, usually for economic and planning reasons. As we outline in Box 1, if strong demand exists within an area for both social and private housing, developers and planners have sometimes decided to build a mixture of housing on the same site. The planning system has allowed local authorities to ensure that a range of housing is built to meet local needs.

As the arguments have grown against concentrating poorer households within neighbourhoods, the impetus for building mixed estates appears to have heightened. In 1997, a government consultation paper on planning and affordable housing noted that,

> 'whilst the primary objective will be to ensure that there is enough housing to meet the agreed needs in quantitative terms, local authorities should also ensure that there is a mix of types of housing to encourage the development of mixed communities'.[24]

Box 1. Pragmatic reasons for building mixed tenure developments

Sometimes, building an estate with a mixture of private and social housing makes good economic sense. For example, if a local authority wants to develop an area for new social housing, selling off some of the land that it owns to a private contractor can help finance the development of local infrastructure and amenities which the social housing tenants need. Occasionally, developers also sell new houses to housing associations if they have problems selling the properties.

Even if a developer has no overriding economic reason for building a mixed development, the local authority may use the planning system to create such a mix because it wants to ensure that local housing needs are met. In 1992, Government planning guidance on house building stated that 'new housing developments of a substantial scale should incorporate a reasonable mix and balance of house types and sizes to cater for a range of housing needs'.[23] This guidance and subsequent statements have been used, in particular, to ensure that social housing is built. If local authorities are able to substantiate the need for more social housing, they are able to make planning consent for a development conditional on including a certain percentage of social housing. Typically, between 10 and 40 per cent of properties on large new developments are required to be put aside for social housing. Occasionally, local authorities have also picked up the idea of catering for a range of housing needs by arguing that more private housing should be built in an area dominated by social housing in order to meet a growing demand for home ownership.

In other words, creating a mix is seen as important *in itself*, not just in order to meet a range of housing needs. This is not a completely new idea. The post-war new towns such as Milton Keynes also had aspirations to create 'balanced communities'. But the aspiration to create a mix is undergoing a particular revival. When new draft guidance was published in the spring of 1999, the emphasis of government policy had further moved towards advocating mix for its own sake. It states that:

> The Government believes that it is important to help create mixed and inclusive communities which offer a choice of housing and

> lifestyle. Local planning authorities should encourage the development of mixed and balanced communities: they should ensure that new housing developments help to secure a better social mix by avoiding the creation of large areas of housing for a particular social or income group. The Government does not accept that different types of housing and tenures make for bad neighbourhoods. Local plans should adopt policies to secure a more appropriate mix of dwelling size, type and affordability in both new developments and conversions to meet the changing composition of households in their area.[25]

That message is also found in a variety of other reports. For example, the White Paper *Planning for the Communities of the Future* noted that, 'the Government is committed to creating mixed communities, wherever appropriate, rather than areas of exclusively high-cost or low-cost housing.'[26] The recently published report by the Urban Task Force was unequivocal. It recommended that,

> 'In all future urban development, and where possible in existing urban areas, we must strive for a much greater mix of building types and housing tenures'

> and 'To avoid single housing tenure, of whatever kind, designs should offer a wide choice of tenure options at urban block, street and neighbourhood level, in a way which does not distinguish tenure by grouping or house type. New development should also be used to bring balance into mono-tenure areas.'[27]

At a more local level, a report on *Affordable Homes for London* by London Pride Partnership, a body which brings together representatives of business, local authorities and voluntary organisations, suggested that a key objective of housing policy should be to 'create homes within vibrant and mixed communities for the diversity of people who make up London's community.'[28] And a number of housing professionals have also recently endorsed the claim that mixed estates are generally better than solely private ones. For example, one report notes that:

> 'the pressures from nominating agencies and from those in housing need can lead to the development of communities which are unbalanced in some terms, whether social, economic, age or household composition. It is not sufficient for associations to claim that this is not their fault; they are acting as social engineers, if only by default. A better approach would be pro-active, seeking to allocate in such a way as to create a variety on the estate similar to that in the neighbouring communities.'[29]

With such a policy emphasis, more housing associations and local authorities appear to be planning mixed tenure developments. Precise figures are difficult to come by – the rhetoric certainly runs far ahead of actual practice – and the motivations behind building such estates are even harder to assess. However, surveys suggest that between one-third and two-thirds of housing associations are interested in developing mixed tenure estates.[30] The pressure is also mounting for local authorities to think through their goals in relation to mix. For example, Parliament's Select Committee on Environment, Transport and Regional Affairs recently stated that 'we strongly recommend that the local authority has a much greater say in the mix of tenure, size, type and density of the houses built.'[31]

If, as these documents advocate, a greater mix results, then the beginning of the twenty-first century could be seen as a turning point in which geographical segregation between rich and poor at the neighbourhood level started to subside. The communities of the future might see richer and poorer households living side by side in a manner which has become less common over the last century as the better off used cheap transport to leave behind undesirable areas and the poor were trapped in large social housing estates.

But implementing such a vision might have considerable costs. The government would have to be more prescriptive about what types of new houses are built in which locations. And if people do not like living in mixed estates extra incentives may be needed. In the rest of this report we therefore aim to develop the debate about the costs and benefits of creating such communities in more detail. In particular, we consider the contentious issue of whether such developments create better local social and cultural environments.

3. Crucial questions about social relations on mixed tenure developments

All of the proposed advantages of mixed areas – to the local economy, image, local services and local society – attract debate. For example, Mark Kleinman of the London School of Economics suggests that the real problems of households in poverty stem primarily from their lack of skills and precarious position in an increasingly competitive global market for workers, rather than the local area in which they live.[32]

More evidence is needed to validate most claims. But as we noted in the last chapter, probably the most contentious issues about mixed tenure estates is whether they create more advantageous social and cultural conditions in a local area compared to single tenure developments. Do they help create a better sort of community and, if so, which types of schemes? Some estates labelled 'mixed tenure' have private and social housing dispersed across them. Others have six foot high walls separating the different types of property. Some are built by the same contractor, others are the result of the development of separate plots of land by different builders. Some are very large – substantial parts of inner cities or greenfield sites. Others comprise only a handfull of houses on a street or two.

Assessing the types of communities that develop on mixed schemes is the focus of this report. To make that assessment manageable, this chapter:

- teases out the social and cultural issues around mixed tenure estates in greater depth – we consider which social and cultural factors must be assessed as policy-makers attempt to evaluate the pros and cons of mixed tenure developments, and

- outlines the extent to which existing research sheds light on these issues. This provides the background for understanding the new primary research that we report in chapters four and five.

The importance of social relations on mixed tenure developments

Crucial questions about mixed communities

Some of most in-depth analysis of the relationship between concentrated deprivation and local social and cultural conditions comes from North America. In the United States neighbourhood deprivation is even more marked than in Britain. The ghettos of large American cities (and their residents) have generated a range of emotions from a sense of injustice, to concern, fear and scorn. Traditionally, North American liberals have emphasised the ways in which these neighbourhoods have suffered from the decline of manufacturing industries, lack of social investment and racial discrimination. Conservatives have put more of the blame on the residents for 'bringing problems on themselves'. Extreme conservatives have raised the idea of a dysfunctional 'underclass' characterised by illegality and illegitimacy who, they believe, constitute the cause of most of the problems of deprivation (despite the fact that the term underclass was originally coined to refer to those who suffered from the effects of economic decline rather than created problems).

The traditional divide between the right and left has, however, become less marked over the last decade. Those on the left have started to say that local cultural and social factors, not just economic ones, are important to the success or failure of neighbourhoods. They believe that although the root cause of neighbourhood decline is usually found in economic problems, particularly unemployment, a concentration of people suffering such problems can *in turn* foster local cultures and societies which exacerbate the problems of a neighbourhood.

William Julius Wilson, a professor of sociology at the University of Harvard, states these ideas succinctly:

> 'I believe that there is a difference, on the one hand, between a jobless family whose mobility is constrained by ... the economy and the larger society but nonetheless lives in an area with a rela-

> tively low rate of poverty, and on the other hand, a jobless family that lives in an inner city ghetto-neighbourhood that is not only influenced by these same constraints but also by the behaviour of other jobless families in the neighbourhood. The latter influence is one of culture.'[33]

He believes that as jobs declined in cities in the north east of the United States during the 1970s and 1980s, the working and middle classes migrated to the suburbs along with the jobs. He suggests that their departure deprived the inner city neighbourhoods not just of money but of role models for children, social support for those in difficulty and informal links to the jobs market. Others suggest that cultures of short termism or a lack of expectation to work can develop in areas with a concentration of those in great poverty.[34]

But many in Britain disagree with such analysis. For example, Bob Holman, the writer and community worker on the Easterhouse estate in Glasgow attacks the idea that richer people may somehow have a better culture. Low income, he suggests, is the main affliction of residents on such estates, not deficient local societies or low aspirations.[35]

The government appears slightly uncertain about whether mixed tenure developments really do directly create tangibly better social and cultural environments. As the quotes in the last chapter indicate, much of the rhetoric about mixed areas implies that such areas have a better sort of community. Terms such as 'thriving' communities, 'balanced' communities, 'vibrant' communities, and 'inclusive' communities crop up in most documents about mixed tenure estates. But it is unclear whether the term 'community' is really used to denote social relationships between different residents or only to identify a group of people who simply share the same space. As one dictionary notes, community is a remarkably elastic term.

> '*Community.* One of the most vague and elusive concepts in social science, community continues to defy precise definition. Part of the problem stems from the diversity of meanings attributed to the term and the emotive overtones it usually conjures up. It is an omnibus word used to describe social units varying from villages,

housing estates and local neighbourhoods to ethnic groups, nations and international organisations.'[36]

By using such a catch-all term, the government has not completely committed itself to whether or not it believes that poorer residents will actually have social contact which enhances their links with the labour market, to other resources and role models as the American literature suggests.

The first question to ask of mixed tenure developments is, therefore, whether they actually promote social and cultural environments that could bring tangible benefits to their residents, in terms of information about jobs, support from neighbours, role models or greater understanding and tolerance between different economic groups.

As importantly, some housing professionals express fears that rather than bringing community benefits, mixing will create tensions between the different tenure groups. As we noted in chapter two, 'the Government does not accept that different types of housing and tenures make bad neighbours.' But others do worry. For example, one housing manager we spoke to stated that

'Estates work better where there is some segregation. It avoids having antagonistic attitudes in relation to the common areas.'

Another noted that

'The mixing of tenures has improved the perception of the estate from the outside, for it isn't perceived as a council estate. It has not made any difference to the people who live there. It has only caused envy'.

A house builder echoed such feelings, saying that they would not enter into a very geographically integrated – 'pepper-potted' – multi-tenure scheme because antagonisms would arise between tenure groups over issues such as whether all residents were paying the same service charges. A government department also expressed reservations about such schemes because district valuers lower their estimated land prices for mixed schemes in anticipation that owners will not want to live in them.

Those who seriously consider mixed tenure are very aware of these issues. For example, one recent conference was asked to consider the proposition that 'the current emphasis on mixed communities is in danger of obscuring the fact that community diversity can create friction as well as harmony'.[37]

The second question to ask of mixed tenure estates is, therefore, whether tensions tend to develop between different tenure groups and, if so, how these tensions can be avoided.

Even if tensions do not develop, others worry that different tenure groups might be unwilling to participate in common community groups. Increasingly, housing managers and other public agency staff are looking to local residents to take some role in preventing and rectifying neighbourhood problems such as crime and environmental damage. For example, neighbourhood watch schemes, residents associations and local community groups have all been promoted as important institutions for increasing the social and economic sustainability of estates. More generally, a key perceived characteristic of successful communities has often been, in the words of one report, 'relationships of trust between those people sharing an identifiable location or space, participation in shared activities and goals, and common use of facilities or amenities.'[38]

These aspirations for housing estates also resonate with an influential strand of sociological research that emphasises the importance of informal social networks in developing trust between different sections of a population and in acting as the catalyst for the development of civic institutions and basis for collective action. For example, the American academic, Robert Putnam, argues that those societies in which formal and informal networks exist between many sections of the population are more economically successful than those which are characterised by narrow social ties, such as domination by family structures.[39] He emphasises the way in which such links enable societies to take collective action to face challenges. A similar view is promoted by the historian Francis Fukuyama. He proposes that diverse networks help increase trust, which in turn reduces the need to use resources on creating complex legal systems, litigation, auditing, policing and or protecting one's own interest.[40]

The third question for mixed tenure developments is, therefore, the extent to which residents from all tenure groups are likely to come together to tackle common problems, so that community action has legitimacy and can harness the resources of all sections of the population.

The existing evidence

Unfortunately, the answers to these questions are largely unknown. Because the number of recent significant studies has been so few it is worth noting them all.

One study considered the success of four estates in west London which have a mixture of shared ownership (part rented, part bought) and social rented properties.[41] The researchers were generally positive about the estates. They concluded that the problems that did occur on the estates – noise, vandalism, disruptive children and the like – had little to do with the mixture of tenures, but were rather just typical problems which arise on most housing estates. They found that the owners and the tenants were generally happy with living on the estates, although many of the owners would prefer to live in a non-mixed scheme, all other things being equal. They also concluded that a small proportion of shared ownership can 'make a measurable difference in terms of the economic and employment profile of the estate',[42] but that more research would be needed to evaluate whether a broader social benefit was achieved.

A second relevant study considered residents' use of time and social contacts on three mixed tenure estates in Scotland.[43] These were all long-standing social housing estates that recently had new private homes built in them. The researchers asked residents of 38 households to fill out diaries. They found that whereas the lives of renters centred on the estate, 'most owners live much of their lives outside the home area and, in 90 per cent of cases, in carrying out activities beyond the estate they were not in contact with other people from the estate.' However, they found that owners often had at least *some* contact with other residents on the estate. They concluded that at least one group of owners could become more embedded in their localities, but that 'this falls well short of the transformation of social relations which is being sought in the debate about social exclusion.'

The impact of mixing tenures also arises in broader studies of new housing developments by Ian Cole and colleagues from the Sheffield Hallam University. One study used focus groups to investigate feelings about mix, among other factors, on four estates in Yorkshire.[44] They found that 'generally residents did not think that tenure mix really mattered, although images of a divide between owners and tenants persisted.'[45] Another found that the diversification of tenure was viewed positively by those working and living on seven estates in the Northeast of England which had been subjected to considerable redevelopment schemes.[46] They suggest that introducing private housing can help improve the image of the estate locally, but could not assess whether mixing tenures led to more inclusive communities or simply reinforced social divisions.

These studies give some insights into particular estates. However, they tend not to be large or regionally diverse enough to draw concrete national conclusions about the social and cultural benefits and the challenges that different sorts of mixed tenure development are likely to generate.

In the remainder of this report, we attempt to answer the most pressing questions about the social and cultural characteristics of mixed tenure developments by drawing on new research. As we noted in the last chapter, the type of community which characterises mixed tenure housing developments is only one factor in considering their merit. The arguments for mix as a way to enhance local economies, the image of the area and local services have always been firmer – although often still not proved – and are certainly as important. But in considering the emphasis on mixed 'communities' which runs through so much discussion of new housing, the social relations that develop between residents of mixed tenure estates are clearly an important element in assessing their benefits or drawbacks. And given that tenure mix is probably going to increase in one form or another, developers and housing managers need to consider which styles of mix are likely to bring particular social benefits or challenges.

4. Prospects for mutual support between residents of different tenures

The positive aspirations for mixed tenure developments – of rich and poor sharing information and other resources, of understanding each other better, of providing role models for local children – all rely on an often taken-for-granted feature of neighbourhoods: that residents get to know each other. In this chapter we test that simple assumption.

Measuring local social contact

Our purpose – a fairly broad investigation into the nature of communities that are developing on mixed tenure estates – required a large number of interviews in order to start drawing general conclusions about such estates. As we noted in the previous chapter, the existing research on social relations in mixed tenure estates tends to be either confined to one region or small in scale. We therefore interviewed 1,000 residents of ten mixed tenure developments across England. Their responses allow us to sketch the contours of interaction on such estates.

Entire neighbourhoods in new towns and other areas have often been planned to include a mixture of housing types, but planning a mix on new estates or roads, as endorsed by the Urban Task Force and other groups, has been less common (sometimes it occurs when councils or housing associations buy properties in existing streets or tenants buy houses through right-to-buy schemes). In order to investigate social relations on mixed tenure estates we therefore had to choose fairly new estates, typically redeveloped between two and eight years ago, together with one or two more established areas.

The estates represent a cross-section of the different types of development that tend to be described as mixed tenure (details are outlined in Box 2). Some have fairly high geographical integration between the tenure types with different tenures on many roads – although usually still in groups – while others confine the tenures to different zones. Some have considerable community support, such as community workers, others have little. Some have their own shops, others do not. They all have at least 150 properties, as we aimed to complete about 100 questionnaires from each.

On larger estates, we tended to survey parts in which owners and tenants had greatest physical proximity and also the longer established parts of the estates. If anything, therefore, some of our details of social contact between different tenures are probably overestimates of estate wide interaction (see Box 3 for details of the survey).

Social contact

Given the relative newness of many residents on the estates, we expected only limited social contact to develop between neighbours. But, as Figure 3 shows, although the majority of respondents had got

Figure 3. Percentage of respondents knowing other residents by name
(Ranked by the proportion knowing any resident with a different tenure)

Estate	Knows anyone	Knows anyone of different tenure	Knows more than 5 people same tenure	Knows more than 5 people of different tenure
Town End Farm	98	60	80	38
Greater Leys	97	56	72	25
Bowthorpe	95	52	73	29
Great Notley	95	41	77	21
Royal Quays	95	38	67	19
Maple Meadow	98	33	65	4
Broomhall	90	27	44	5
Bonamy	92	24	57	13
Windmill Park	89	21	57	4
Bordesley	91	19	48	8
Average	94	37	64	17

Note: for the purpose of the research we divided residents into three tenures, social housing (housing association or local authority), shared ownership and ownership. We asked the approximate number of people that they knew with each ownership or rental arrangement.

Box 2. The estates

1. **Royal Quays** a fairly large housing redevelopment on an old industrial and docks site on the north shore of the Tyne, about ten miles from the centre of Newcastle. Most of the streets in the area which we studied were built about five years ago and contain a mixture of social and private housing.
2. **Town End Farm** a large 1960s local authority estate on the edge of Sunderland which had new private housing built in small groups throughout the estate at the beginning of the 1990s and has had extensive renovations to the local authority stock and some transfer of stock to a housing association over the last eight years.
3. **Broomhall** a five year old development of about 300 flats and houses near the centre of Sheffield, with private and social housing predominantly focused on different sides of the estate but with some sections of greater integration. The site was previously a council estate whose properties suffered structural problems.
4. **Bowthorpe Village** a large, relatively self-contained area of mixed housing and extensive amenities on the edge of Norwich which has been gradually developed since the late 1970s.
5. **Bordesley Urban Village** a number of small housing developments in an area of inner city Birmingham which once had a considerable mix of industry and housing and has been extensively redeveloped with environmental, community and economic improvements as well as new housing.
6. **Greater Leys** a recent extension to the 1960s Blackbird Leys estate on the edge Oxford, including zones of new social, shared ownership (partly rented from a housing association, partly bought) and private housing which join on some streets.
7. **Great Notley Village** a large greenfield housing development with many supporting amenities near Braintree, Essex, which has a fairly small proportion of social housing scattered in some parts of it.
8. **Windmill Park** a new housing development on the site of an old hospital near Ealing, west London, with private and social rented housing very segregated and a smaller number of shared ownership properties in the social housing section.
9. **Bonamy estate** a redeveloped large local authority estate in Southwark, inner south London, with very separate sections of private, shared ownership, local authority and housing association properties, mostly new and some renovated.
10. **Maple Meadow** a small greenfield development on the edge of Plympton, near Plymouth, with one street dominated by rented social housing, one with a mix, a couple with shared ownership and a small separate section of private housing – only joined by a small path.

Full details of the estates are given in appendix one.

Box 3. The survey

In deciding which houses to survey, our aim was to balance three criteria:

- focus the research on the longer established parts of the estates, in which residents would have had more time to meet
- focus the research, where possible, on roads which had a mixture of private and social housing
- interview a significant proportion of residents from all tenure groups.

Within these criteria we chose a random sample of properties which were visited up to four times until a response or refusal was given. Full details of the survey are given in appendix two.

With these criteria we gained an insight into the views and experiences of residents of all tenures who had lived on the estates long enough to meet neighbours of a different tenure. They did not, however, ensure that the views will necessarily be representative of all residents on the estate. For example, the views of residents in some of the newer sections are likely to be under-represented.

Compared to the entire British population, respondents tended to be relatively young. About half were under 35, probably reflecting the large proportion of first-time buyers and young families on these developments. Two-thirds were women, probably reflecting their greater propensity to be in when interviewers called. The proportion of professional, managerial and administrative workers was similar to that of the national population, but fewer households were headed by skilled manual workers and more were solely reliant on state benefits. Apart from Bordesley Urban Village, Broomhall, Bonamy and Windmill Park, the vast majority of respondents were white.

to know the names of more than five other residents, many did not know the name of even one other resident with a different tenure.

On some estates (or, to be more precise, the parts of the estates which we surveyed), levels of interaction were almost non-existent. On Windmill Park, less than one in ten of the owner occupiers we interviewed knew any residents of social housing or with a shared ownership arrangement despite being in a block which is surrounded by such housing (albeit separated by a road and railings in most parts).

These findings were often echoed in our interviews with those people who particularly knew the areas. For example, a typical comment in Bordesley Urban Village, the area in which our respondents recorded least interaction between different tenures, was that 'there's nothing to bring people together here ... It will be the children that begin mixing if it ever happens at all.' In Bordesley the local authority and community groups had tried to foster a notion of urban village, for example with a 'village hall' and a community worker. However, most of the people who we spoke to suggested that, in particular, the new owners mainly led their social and working lives outside the area and had little reason to interact with other residents of the neighbourhood, particularly with those in social housing. Many of the long-standing residents, usually those in social housing, stated that they never saw any of the newer owner occupiers. The reasons given by the long-standing residents of the social housing varied from suggestions that owners had so much debt with their mortgages that they could not afford to go out to local pubs to a view that they went everywhere in cars.

This is not to say that certain cross-tenure groups do not meet in most estates. For example, in Bowthorpe, one of the longer established estates, a whole host of local groups exist which include residents of all tenures: a church, mothers and toddler's groups, youth groups, a cinema club, sports clubs. And in some places, those with particular knowledge of the area believed that tenure was little barrier to interaction. For example, one community worker we spoke to in Royal Quays (which has average interaction according to our survey) perceived the estate to be very much one community. She noted that,

> 'Walking down the street, you would not know the difference between an owner and a renter, even if you spoke to them'.
>
> *Questioner:* 'Is that because houses cost less to buy here?'
>
> 'No, I think it is just because people don't have that prejudice about being a renter or an owner. On the residents association we have a similarly mixed participation of all the tenures. People are very close in this community. We also have some successful pro-

fessionals on the estate – we have chief executives of local authorities and people high up in the universities.'

But the general picture is clear: only a minority of residents have got to know people of other tenures in the typical developments which are currently described as 'mixed tenure'.

Mutual support

This pattern of relatively low interaction between residents of different tenures was repeated in the level of mutual support between tenure groups. Overall, less than one in five respondents said that they could ask any resident with a different tenure for help or advice with a variety of minor needs, although the majority could rely on at least somebody of the same tenure. Different tenure groups do not generally appear to be finding great synergies in their resources – such as between those with time and those with money – or helping each other out.

Figure 4. Proportion relying on other residents help or advice

Type of help or advice	From anyone on estate	From someone with a different tenure
Lending and borrowing (if you needed tools, or a cup of sugar)	56%	9%
Transport (for example if you wanted a lift somewhere)	39%	7%
Shopping (would you ask people to bring you things back from the shops)	36%	6%
DIY and gardening	26%	6%
Childcare and baby sitting	23%	5%
Problems at work	15%	4%
Getting help with filling in forms	14%	4%
Finding a job	13%	4%
Getting advice about money	10%	4%
Any of the above	69%	17%

Influences on interaction

These two findings – of less than two-fifths of residents having any contact with neighbours of different tenures and less than one-fifth actually sharing resources and information – suggest typically limited social contact has emerged on the types of mixed tenure estate that have been built in Britain over the past decade. Yet as the figures for individual estates (Figure 3) indicated, these average figures mask very considerable variation. For instance, the proportion of residents who knew other residents with a different tenure varied from less than 20 per cent up to 60 per cent. That threefold variation suggests that planners and housing managers might be able to foster greater social interaction in the future should they wish to.

Box 4 (over) indicates those factors which appear to be significantly associated with interaction between different tenure groups. The actual degree of correlation was fairly low for all factors. Interaction appears to be influenced by a variety of factors rather than just one or two key determinants.

Some indication of the strength of association between certain attributes and social interaction is also shown by Figure 5.

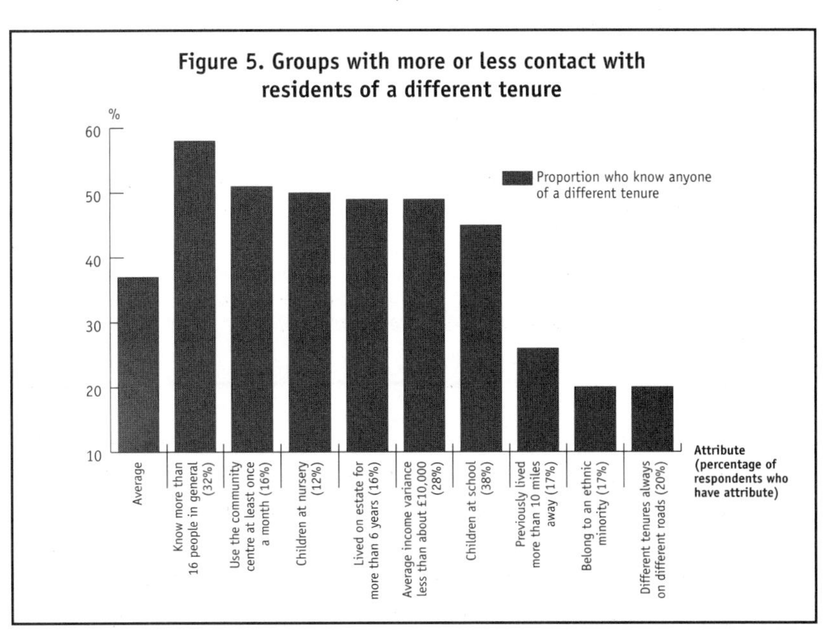

Box 4. Factors associated social interaction between tenure groups

Which factors are significant (ranked by degree of correlation)
How many residents the respondent knew in general (irrespective of tenure)
Degree of geographical segregation between tenures on the respondent's estate
Average differences in income between different tenure groups on estate
Whether belong to an ethnic minority (less interaction)
Whether used the community centre frequently
How long had lived on the estate
Whether previously lived nearby
Whether have children attending school
Whether have children attending play group

Borderline significance
How often use the local park
How often use the local newsagent

Not significant
Age of respondent
Gender of respondent
Number of people in household
Whether working or not
How often use local supermarkets
How often use local pub
How often use the local post office
How often go to a church or other place of worship

Note: We use a composite measure of interaction based whether respondents knew any or some residents of a different tenure and whether they could ask for help or advice from someone with a different tenure. [47] The levels of correlation were generally small – from 0.1 to 0.2 – with the exception of how many residents respondents knew in total (0.4). Some of the degrees of correlation decline if other factors are taken into account. For example, those who use community centres are also slightly more likely to have children. In particular, those estates with high physical segregation are also likely to have higher degrees of income inequality between the different tenure groups.

These help give a rough idea of potential influences. Because influences overlap they should not be interpreted as the precise levels of influence of different factors. For example, those who use a community centre are also more likely to have children at nursery school, so it is hard to disentangle the relative levels of influence of each. However, combing this statistical analysis with the responses to other questions and our more in-depth interviews allows us to draw some general conclusions about influences on social contact between residents of different tenures.

1. *The biggest single barrier to contact is that properties of different tenure tend to be on different streets or different parts of streets.* In the words of one housing manager:

> 'The physical separation of the tenures means there is not much interaction. Even having different tenures on different streets can create segregation'

Figure 6 shows why. Most people only get to know their next door neighbours or people they bump into on the street (usually near their home). Usually, respondents would say that they only knew the others in their part of the street or close. Given that most 'mixed tenure'

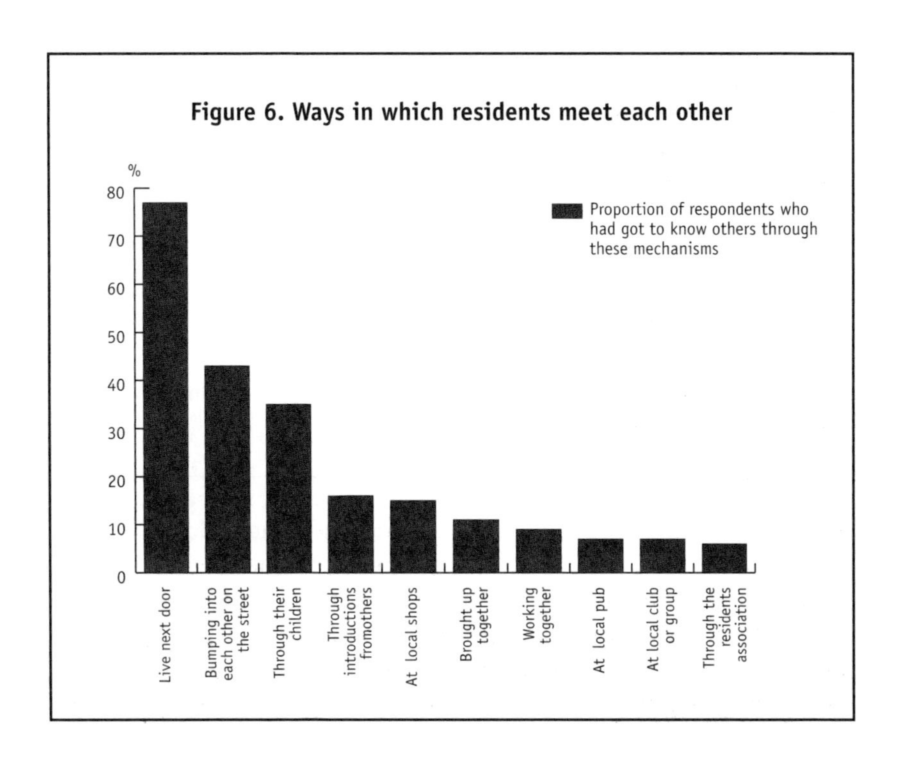

Figure 7. Proportion who knew the name of anybody from a different tenure, by degree of integration

Category	Estates	Proportion who knew anyone of another tenure
Considerable road sharing	Town End Farm Royal Quays Great Notley Village	46%
Some shared roads	Greater Leys Maple Meadow Broomhall Bowthorpe	43%
Segregated roads / different blocks	Windmill Park Bordesley	20%
Poor access to different tenure blocks	Bonamy	24%

estates are not mixed at the level of parts of streets it is unsurprising that tenure groups mix little.

Even the figures for those estates with considerable road sharing (noted in Figure 7) include some responses from people who lived on mono-tenure roads and others who lived at the far end of the street from the different tenure properties. Our findings suggest that in a truly 'pepper potted' arrangement of private and social housing, most residents know people of another tenure.

2. Compared to physical segregation, income differences are less important

Estates with lower average income differences between tenure groups did have slightly greater social interaction between residents of different tenure than estates with large income differences (using a very crude measure of average incomes[48]). And interaction between shared owners – a 'middle' category of tenure – and full owners and tenants was often greater than between residents of those two tenures. However, the correlation with income variation is largely explained by the fact that estates with large income differences tend be more physically separated. We would still expect the majority of residents in very geographically integrated streets to have some contact with those of another tenure, even if the income differences were large. That will, of course, also depend on other factors such as whether residents live in blocks of flats or more accessible houses.

3. Schools and nursery schools are by far the most important local amenity for meeting other people, and if residents meet any other residents through them they are fairly likely to meet residents of another tenure. But a significant minority of parents still do not meet any other estate residents through their children's school.

One nursery school worker we spoke to summed up the social role of the nursery in the following terms:

> 'In many ways the nursery is a catalyst for families coming together. Because of the mixed tenure, you've had some single parents moving in to the rented properties and you have had families moving into the shared ownership and buying their own properties. The common denominator was the groups for people who had or were having children. So the nursery was, in many respects, the main catalyst for the meeting of different families.'

More people meet fellow estate residents through their children than any other way except being next door neighbours or bumping into each other on the street. And as Figure 5 indicated, half of parents with

Figure 8. Role of school in meeting other residents

56% have no children at school or nursery school

16% have children at school or nursery but know nobody on the estate through their children

28% have got to know other residents of the estate through the school or nursery. Of these:

- 14% had got to know parents with another tenure
- 8% were clear they had not got to know parents with a different tenure
- 6% were unsure about the tenure of the other residents they met at school

children at nursery knew estate residents of another tenure. Also, for some parents tenure is just not an issue at the school gate – they did not know whether the parents they met had different tenures or not.

Yet possibly a more surprising finding is that while schools and nurseries bring many together, over a third of parents do not meet any other residents through their child's school or play group (see Figure 8). Even this 'catalyst for meeting' is outside the experience of many residents.

4. Other local facilities and amenities can be visited frequently, but are rarely places to meet people for the first time

As Figure 9 shows, many local shops and amenities are used fairly frequently by residents. But almost nobody meets people for the first time through these facilities: 7 per cent of respondents reportedly met people in the local pub, 7 per cent in local clubs and 15 per cent in local shops. That does not mean that such places have no social role. But their social function is more to cement relationships with existing friends and acquaintances rather than as forums to meet new people.

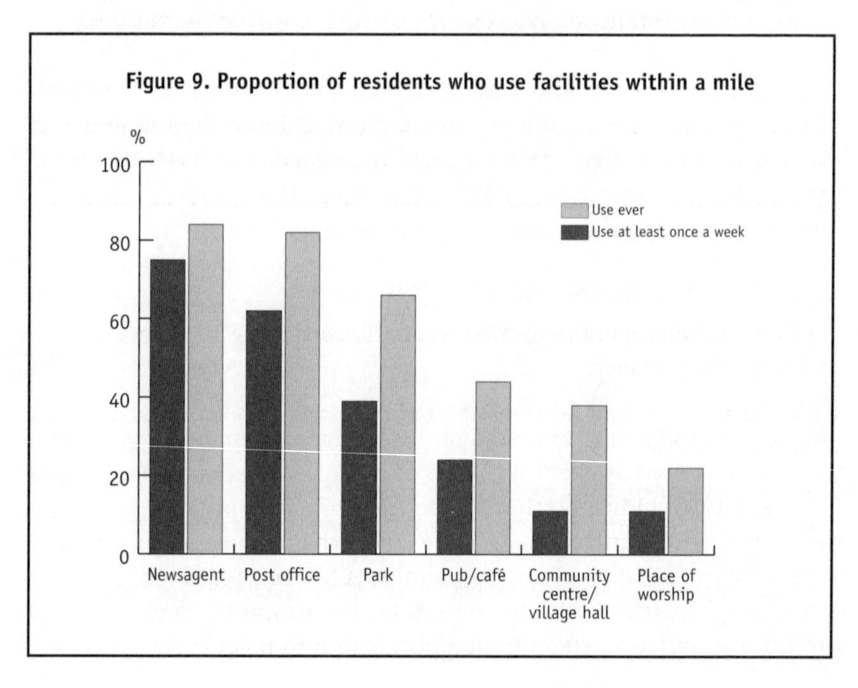

We also found that people who did meet residents of the same tenure through the local pub, or local shops and clubs also tended to know more residents of other tenures. That supports the proposition of point 2, that income difference is not usually a great barrier in itself, just that estate-wide community is generally weak.

5. Community centres do bring residents together, including those of different tenures in many estates, but are frequently only used by a minority of residents

Most surveys of community centres find little use by the general population. For example, when residents were recently asked their views about social and community facilities on six new estates, only between 1 and 11 per cent of residents said that they personally benefited from the facilities.[49] Likewise, a recent anthropological study of a long established urban neighbourhood concluded that 'locations such as the church and a luncheon club are important for the very small numbers that actually attend but hardly impinge any more on the street as a whole'.[50]

Mixed tenure estates are no exception. In the words of one person we spoke to:

> 'When we first moved here we did a survey of the residents and we had a good response rate of people telling us what they wanted to see happening at the community centre. However, the extraordinary thing was how so many people had no idea where we were situated. The committee produce a quarterly A4 news letter about what is happening at the hall, different events, different clubs, what's happening locally, and still people say, "We never knew you were here".'

The community centres in Bonamy, Greater Leys and Bordesley had never been entered by over four-fifths of our respondents.

Yet as Figure 5 indicates, those 16 per cent of the population who do use a community centre at least once a month are considerably more likely to know residents of another tenure. A few centres genuinely act as points of focus for the whole estate. For example, Royal Quays community centre started off in a portacabin to meet certain needs and now has a centre which almost a fifth of respondents in Royal Quays use at least once a week. And community centres can appeal to both owners and tenants. Roughly equal proportions of owners, shared owners and social housing tenants used community centres.

If that success were replicated more generally, interaction would probably be considerably boosted. If not, centres will remain of marginal impact on most estates.

6. The standard demographic characteristics of residents make little difference to cross-tenure interaction, apart from ethnicity

Age, gender and working status had no significant impact on patterns of interaction with residents of different tenure interaction among our respondents (possibly due to survey bias – see note).[51] Working locally was associated with higher contact. So was ethnicity.

Four estates had significant proportions of ethnic minorities: Windmill Park, Broomhall, Bordesley and Bonamy. These estates all had relatively low interaction between the tenures. But in all of them apart from Bonamy, members of ethnic minorities have less cross-tenure mixing than those who describe themselves as white. For example, in Bordesley (in which over two-fifths are members of ethnic minority groups), 27 per cent of white respondents had some cross-tenure contact, compared to only 14 per cent among members of ethnic minorities. That might partly be explained because members of ethnic minorities tended to know fewer people in the estate in general, although they usually have as many people on the estate they can rely on for help or advice and spend similar amounts of time socialising with other residents to white people.

7. Contact is likely to increase over time, but broad-based inclusive communities may never develop on some estates

As Figure 10 indicates, both contact with residents of the same tenure and different tenures rises with length of residency. Likewise, those who lived nearby before moving to the estate are more likely to have contact with those of different tenures. Those who know any other estate residents from childhood are also more likely to know other residents of a different tenure. Yet we can not be confident that really strong inclusive local communities will ever involve the majority of

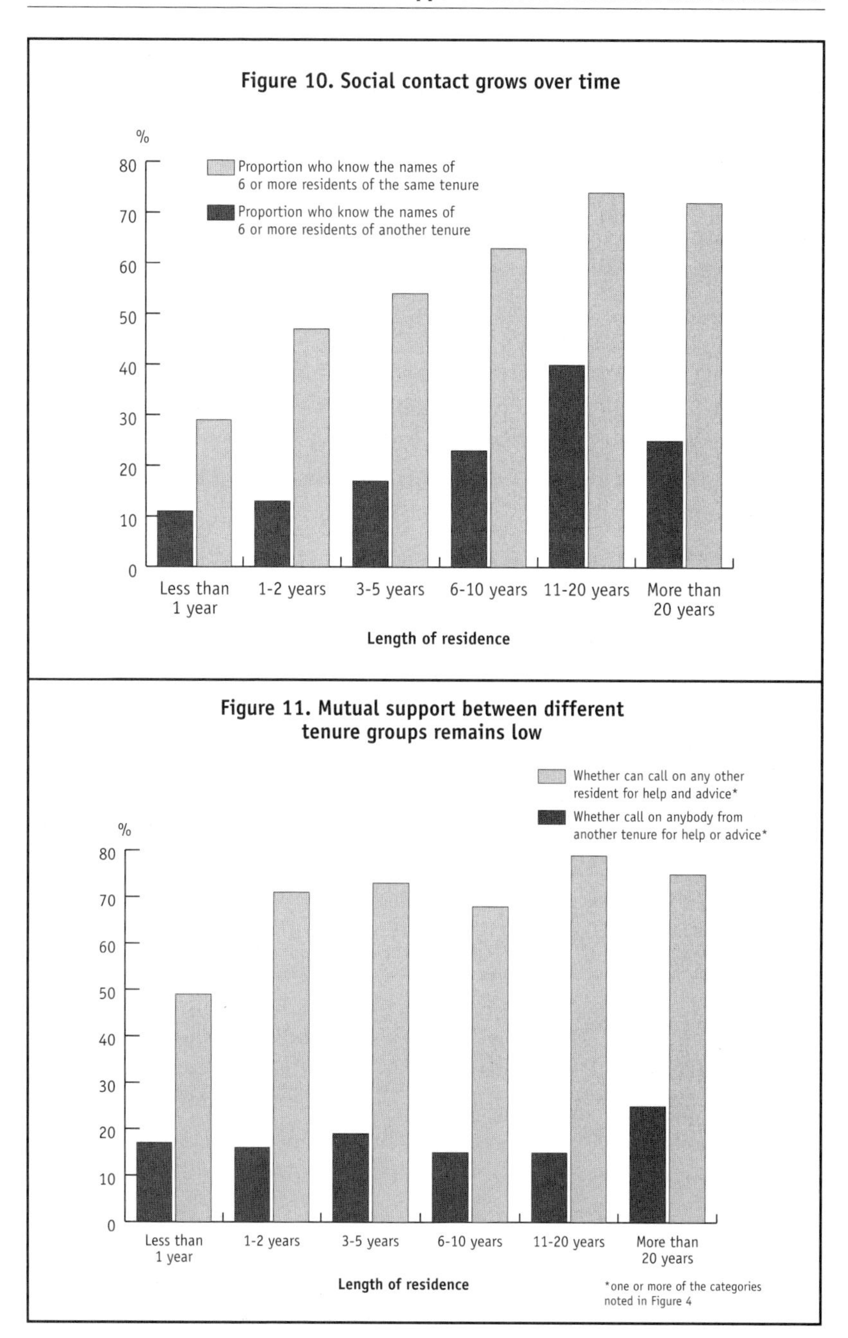
Figure 10. Social contact grows over time
%
80
70
60
50
40
30
20
10
0
Proportion who know the names of 6 or more residents of the same tenure
Proportion who know the names of 6 or more residents of another tenure
Less than 1 year
1-2 years
3-5 years
6-10 years
11-20 years
More than 20 years
Length of residence
Figure 11. Mutual support between different tenure groups remains low
Whether can call on any other resident for help and advice*
Whether call on anybody from another tenure for help or advice*
%
80
70
60
50
40
30
20
10
0
Less than 1 year
1-2 years
3-5 years
6-10 years
11-20 years
More than 20 years
Length of residence
*one or more of the categories noted in Figure 4

residents. As Figure 11 indicates, mutual support between tenure groups remains low even after many years.

Implications

The nature of community on housing estates – focused on near neighbours

Our first question about mixed tenure developments, raised in chapter three, was

> 'Whether they actually promote social and cultural environments which could bring tangible benefits to their residents, in terms of information about jobs, support from neighbours or role models and greater understanding and tolerance between different economic groups.'

Such benefits rely on social contact between residents with different economic circumstances.

Our study sought to consider the extent of social contact within the context of overall levels of estate-wide social contact. The findings suggest that relatively few estate-wide communities exist in general, between residents of the same or different tenures. For example, two out of five respondents reported that none of their socialising was with other estate residents (see Figure 12). And only a third said that they knew the names of more than fifteen other people on their estate.

Figure 12. Proportion of socialising spent with other residents

Amount of socialising spent with other residents*	Social housing tenants	Shared owners	Owner occupiers	Average
All	6	2	2	4
Most	13	8	8	11
Some	20	21	18	19
Little	26	17	23	24
None	35	52	46	41

* Question: 'What proportion of your time spent on leisure activities is spent with people from the estate?'

Some studies of other estates claim to find stronger local communities. One recent study of four deprived neighbourhoods characterised the communities as having dense webs of relationships, trust and familiarity.[52] The relative newness of some of our estates will certainly have reduced such estate-wide communities developing. But a broad review of local social relations suggests that the pattern of interaction on our estates is relatively common and that studies which find very dense and close estate-wide networks are the exception.

For example, one review noted the following key features of networks:[53]

1. Community ties are narrow, specialised relationships, not broadly supportive ties – the networks only usually provide a few types of help.
2. People are not wrapped up in traditional densely-knit, tightly bounded communities, but are manoeuvring in sparsely knit, loosely bounded, frequently changing networks. For example, only one-third of members of one person's network typically know each other.
3. Communities have moved out of neighbourhoods to be dispersed networks (but local relations can be important for some things – controlling land use, domestic safety, getting goods and services quickly).
4. Private intimacy has replaced public solidarity.
5. Communities have become domesticated and feminised, focused less on the public male world, and more around meeting in the more female home.

As another study of networks in a part of London noted, 'active communities do exist but at a metropolitan scale in the form of individual, complex, ramifying social networks ... communities are found but are not tied to the residential neighbourhood.'[54]

Our survey suggests that the main loci for estate contact are people's near neighbours. The vast majority know a number of their neighbours. It is neighbours who people say hello to on the street, because they see them and know where they come from. It is near neighbours who people rely upon for occasional help and advice – seven out of ten

Figure 13. Schematic pattern of interaction – likelihood of contact declines quickly with distance

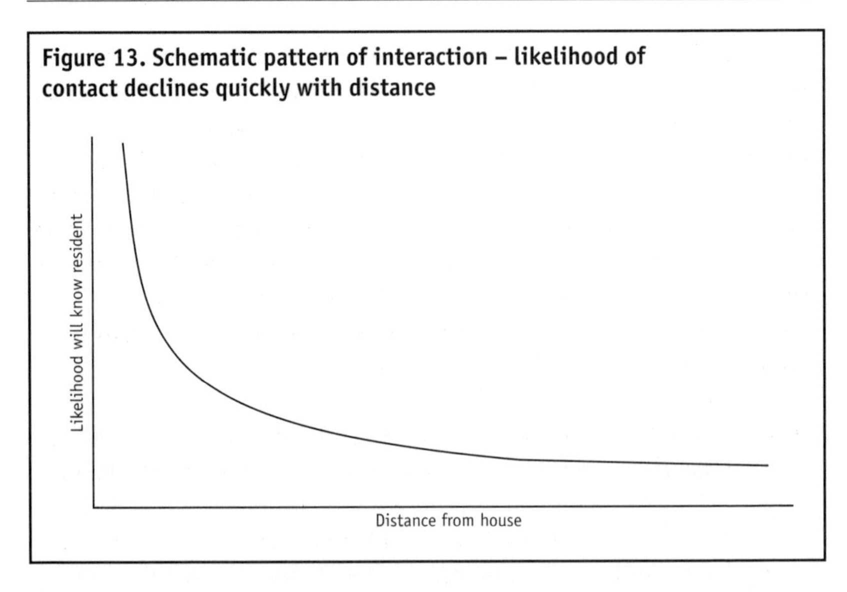

can rely on other estate residents for some form of help or advice. They are usually not great friends, but they play some useful roles.

In this context, it is probably unsurprising that most residents of mixed tenure *estates* know relatively few residents of another tenure: they tend to be separated into different streets or a least different parts of a street. That is not to deny that tenure can be a slight extra barrier. We occasionally came across comments such as, 'The people on the other side of the street [owners] just don't want to know. There's one woman I say hello to, but I think the rest look down on us.' However, we found considerably higher social contact on estates with street level mixing of properties. Our findings suggest that more than half of owners and renters will have cross-tenure contact when they live on streets with a reasonable proportion of both types.

It follows that by far the most important activity to foster social contact between tenure groups will be street-level mixing. Considerable attention is sometimes given to the ideal proportions of different types of tenure on an *estate*. That may be important for the image of the estate or for an estate's local economy (presuming that the local economy works at an estate level), but is far less relevant for social mixing because most housing estates are not social entities in themselves. Instead, planners and housing managers should focus on creating a reasonable balance within each street, or parts of streets.

Fostering social mix beyond near neighbours – an uphill struggle
When people have networks beyond the street – knowing over fifteen others is a good proxy – social contact with residents from other tenures is considerably higher. That is consistent with other findings that tenure, in itself, is usually only a minor barrier to social contact. But the sum total of all the graphs and tables of findings that we have outlined in this chapter is that fostering estate-wide contact is difficult.

The only really important factors increasing contact are having a child at school, longevity of residence and successful community centres. As Figure 14 shows, long residence is associated with social contact between residents in general. Very gradually, people get to know each other through mutual acquaintances. Visiting a community centre and having children also appears to kick-start that. In contrast, the use of pubs, cafés, shops, parks and sports centres are not, in themselves, significant. They are not places for meeting anybody very much, of the same or a different tenure. Nor does allocations policy appear to

Figure 14. Proportion of group knowing more than 15 others

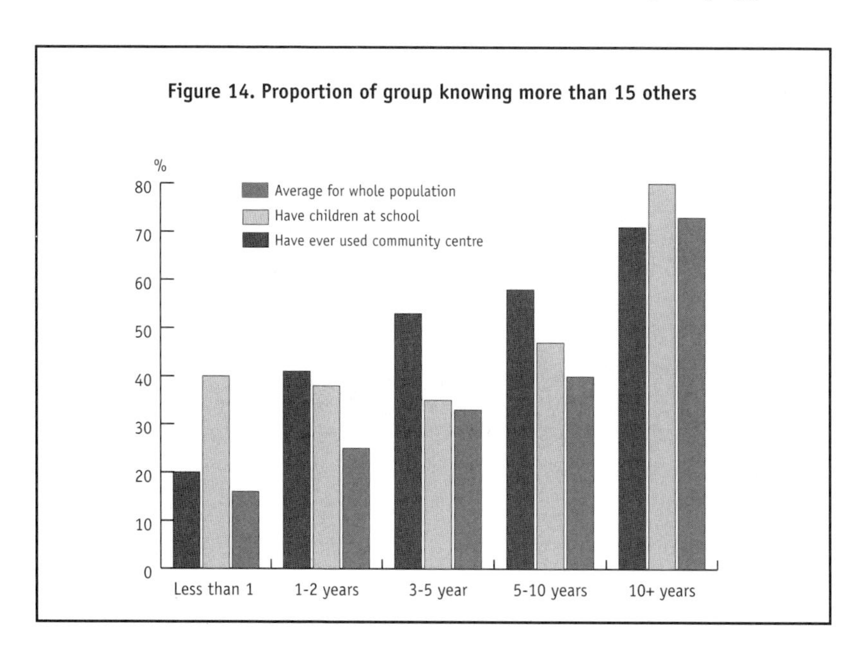

influence social contact, apart from having children on the estate whose numbers most housing managers are wary of increasing. In sum, the process evolves only very slowly or has to be actively facilitated through a community centre.

Beyond longevity and community centres, it is hard to see how the government might foster social interaction. Traditional drivers of convergence have often been shared adversity, a shared enemy (often the local authority) or geographical immobility – none of which policy-makers would be particularly keen to promote. Probably the only way in which people are going to really come together is because they discover they have a common interest. As Figure 15 shows, most people in Britain do not think that they have much in common with their neighbours.

The third of respondents with children who did not know any other parents on the estate are a group who might want to get to know others

Figure 15. How much would you say you have in common with the following?

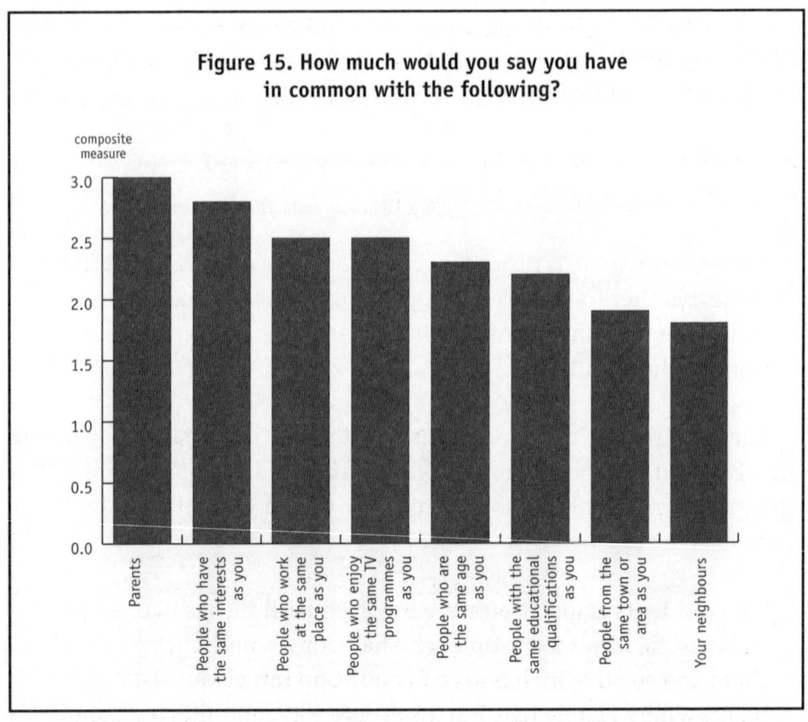

Source: Henley Centre for Forecasting, 1998, *Planning for Social Change*, Henley Centre, London.

because their children act as a common interest. And easy information swapping between residents with free noticeboards in local shops (which our survey suggests are used a lot), local newsheets and local Internet pages covering groups of adjacent streets might also help residents find others with common interests.

So, community centres and information sharing should help. But, overall, we conclude that estate-wide community is unlikely to be a great feature of most parts of Britain in the future without considerable rises in people's typical length of residence in a street. The traditional inner-city mixed communities which William Julius Wilson and others describe bound residents of whole neighbourhoods together through generations of contact, shared places of work, ethnicity, common challenges and local institutions. These conditions are relatively unlikely ever to spontaneously evolve on many mixed tenure estates, just as they have not in many non mixed estates. We therefore conclude that the common style of mixing tenures on the same estate but keeping them on different roads is unlikely to lead to the benefits of sharing resources, role models, greater understanding and links to the labour market which some people hope for.

Implications for social capital – continued possibilities for action

Our third question about mixing was,

> 'the extent to which residents from all tenure groups are likely to come together to tackle common problems, so that community action has legitimacy and can harness the resources of all sections of the population.'

The experience of our estates reinforces the idea that resident involvement can be important. For example, as the following quote illustrates, residents' associations can tackle sometimes small but important issues.

> 'The residents association were involved with things like the provision of facilities for people who had dogs, where they can walk them and so on, which is actually quite an important issue in places where people live. But also there was a monitoring panel

> which worked closely with the residents association. They tended to pass issues between them. For instance there was the issue of television aerials which was initially brought to the attention of the residents association. There was a new system employed that had houses connected to the aerials via underground cables, but the reception was atrocious. It sounds fairly inconsequential, but these things matter to residents. This issue was passed on to the monitoring panel since it was a developmental issue, and was resolved through them.'

As we noted in chapter three, one of the themes of contemporary political sociology is an emphasis on informal social networks as loci of collective action and trust within a society. Sometimes people refer to such connections, and membership of more formal community groups, as 'social capital', conveying the sense that such social structures help the productivity of a group of people.

If we believe that common action is best forged on the roots of informal contact, then our findings suggest that prospects for estate-wide collective action are fairly low. Most residents do not have informal social networks which span across estates and their different tenure groups. However, the actual experience of our estates suggests that while collective action may be somewhat hampered by residents having different landlords and tenures, it can arise quite independently of regular social contact, particularly if some structures or key individuals exist.

For example, in three estates, owners who generally did not know each other much had got together and changed the maintenance and estate management contractors when perceived service got to an unacceptable level. On one, the vast majority of owners had got together, elected a few representatives who dismissed the firm who were responsible for the upkeep of the shared areas, greenery and so on (having been given the contract when the estate was built), and found a new contractor. That included estates such as Broomhall in which the 93 per cent of owners knew less than ten other residents in total. When just a few people take the lead around what is perceived to be a real problem, residents can get together irrespective of their previous contact.

Further, the residents who run 'community action', often quite successfully, tend to be a very small section of the population. For example, in Bowthorpe Village a 'community power' forum brings together a handful of interested residents who feed views into the local council. Their views may not be entirely representative, but they are fairly useful for feeding up factual information, for somewhat increasing pressure on providers of local services and business, and if a big issue came up they would probably act as important point of focus for a much wider section of the population.

In general, then, we found that people will often come together to tackle a problem if they believe it is genuinely common, serious and immediate. What they need is some sort of structure which helps them. That might be a motivated individual or residents association or even a more official community development worker. For example, on two estates we met people who had tried to set up neighbourhood watch groups without any success in the past, but when a specific problem had occurred people became interested. These groups will probably fold once the specific issues are resolved. Yet having the person is a great resource because they will still be a focus for action if big issues re-surface. On other estates, residents groups had grown rapidly when the estate was redeveloped, but withered to a small handful of people afterwards. Yet, because the structure remains, they will be able to grow again if needed. These structures – sometimes fairly inactive – are often more important as indicators of social capital than for the number of active participants or social networks.

Likewise, we should not necessarily worry if membership of community representative associations is low. After all, the vast majority of residents are happy with where they live (see chapter five). What is important is that individuals and groups can be re-activated if specific problems arise, and that they feel they can quickly achieve some sort of influence.

The challenge then for community development is probably to:

- help maintain a few structures or motivated individuals – possibly semi-dormant – who can come together if serious problems arise, and

- circulate information which keep residents informed about problems and builds some sense of collective interest.

Given our findings of little overall social contact and the way in which social networks tend to be generally focused around specific activities rather than tight communities, these seem more realistic goals for stimulating collective action than fostering social contact in general. The extent to which problems arise on mixed estates that need such action in the first place is the issue we turn to in the next chapter.

5. Tensions on mixed tenure estates

With little contact between residents of social and private housing on the majority of existing mixed tenure estates, policy-makers may be concerned that the potential benefits of a more inclusive and integrated society are not being realised. But the other potential benefits from mixed tenure developments – to the image of an area, to local services and to the local economy – are still likely to make them attractive. Our findings also suggest that a more inclusive local society could be fostered if it is recognised that local social networks are very local indeed and tenures are integrated at the street level. In that context, the issue of whether tensions develop between the residents of different tenure groups when they live close together is crucial. If mixing different tenure groups together causes particular problems, not only will they be less than satisfactory places for residents of both tenures to live but housing managers may have to commit more resources to them and house-builders are going to be less likely to invest in building them, fearing that the properties will be difficult to sell. If tensions do not develop, the broader benefits of a mixed area may well be sufficient reason to build such estates.

In this chapter we consider whether the residents of mixed tenure estates perceive problems with their estates and specifically whether tensions appear to be developing between the different groups.

Mixed tenure estates: problem free?

Much of the literature on mixed tenure developments suggest that these estates avoid some of the problems of neighbourhood decline which mono-tenure social housing estates have often faced.[55]

In our estates we generally heard relatively good reports about levels of crime. And the physical environments of most of the estates we studied was generally quite high. Some were considerable successes. For example, Town End Farm on the outskirts of Sunderland once had, in the words of one resident, 'a general feeling that we were at the end of everything. There didn't seem to be any hope.' Now it has a long waiting list for the council properties and people are generally very happy living on the estate. Most of that is due to the general environmental improvements to the estate, but the new private housing probably made some impact on the perception of the estate. Royal Quays had initially been called Royal Ridges because it was so close to the notorious Meadowell estate, known locally as The Ridges. But that image has been lost. House builders' endorsement of the estate is demonstrated by their enthusiastic completion of all the final stages of the development.

Many respondents to our survey rated their estate or local neighbourhood quite highly. Overall, about 65 per cent of owners reported that living on the estate was 'pretty good' or that they 'really like it', as did about 60 percent of shared owners, and just over half of social housing tenants. Only 8 per cent of owner occupiers and shared owners and 13 per cent of residents of social housing said that they 'did not like it' or 'could not stand it'. The remainder said that living on the estate was 'generally all right'.

Yet our survey also suggests that the mixed estates we studied are not all problem free, at least in the perceptions of their residents. As Figure 16 shows, on issues such as security, noise and friendliness, both social housing and private housing residents of mixed tenure estates appeared to view their estates slightly less positively than the respondents to a random national survey of 2,000 people. (The figures show the net proportion of the population who rated the features of the estate positively: those who thought that the estate was good minus those who thought the estate bad.)

Some aspects of our estates were rated more highly that social housing estates in general, such as the cleanliness of the estate, maintenance of buildings, greenery and architectural design. And the slightly lower than average overall satisfaction may have some simple explanations. One explanation may be that satisfaction tends to rise

Figure 16. Perceptions of mixed estates and other estates and neighbourhoods in Britain* (net satisfaction)**

Feature	Social housing mixed tenure	Social housing nationally	Private housing mixed tenure	Private housing nationally	Shared ownership mixed tenure
Security	+ 28	+ 42	+ 40	+ 54	+ 31
Noise	+ 26	+ 44	+ 50	+ 53	+ 36
Graffiti/vandalism	+ 30	+ 33	+ 35	+ 54	+ 55
Cleanliness	+ 31	+ 20	+ 35	+ 39	+ 40
Maintenance	+ 30	+ 20	+ 15	+ 53	- 5
Greenery	+ 40	+ 14	+ 42	+ 57	+ 2
Architecture	+ 33	+ 1	+ 51	+ 23	+ 43
Privacy	+ 34	+ 53	+ 53	+ 69	+ 52
Transport	+ 61	+ 35	+ 60	+ 44	+ 38
Friendly	+ 45	+ 62	+ 47	+ 71	+ 47
Overall***	+ 38	+50	+ 57	+ 73	+ 51

* When respondents did not live on an estate they were asked about their 'immediate neighbourhood – within five minutes walk of their house'.

** The rankings are the net figures of positive or negative responses, derived by subtracting the proportion negative about the estate from those positive.

*** The net overall figure is the percentage who rated living on their estate as 'pretty good' or 'I really like it' minus the percentage who 'do not like it' or 'can not stand it'.

with time. Because residents were relatively new on our estates, we would expect satisfaction to be lower than national averages. Another factor may be income. Satisfaction tends to decline with income.[56] Our estates, with a high proportion of first time buyers and newly allocated social housing tenants (who tend to be those in greatest need), tend to have residents with below average incomes.

These are not, therefore figures to suggest enormous problems. As Figure 17 (over) shows social housing tenants living on mixed tenure estates tend to be more positive about their estate than typical social housing tenants within inner city areas. But the overall satisfaction scores do warn us against complacency and, in particular, a few estates have substantial minorities of dissatisfied residents (Figure 18 over).

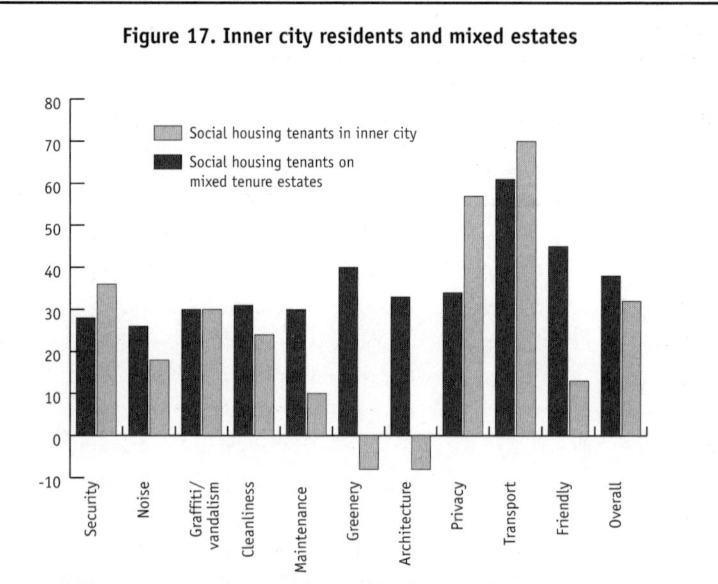

1. The rankings are the net figures of positive or negative responses, derived by subtracting the proportion negative about the estate from those positive.
2. Most of the mixed estates were not inner city. The comparison is purely to illustrate the difference with those estates which typically have most problems.

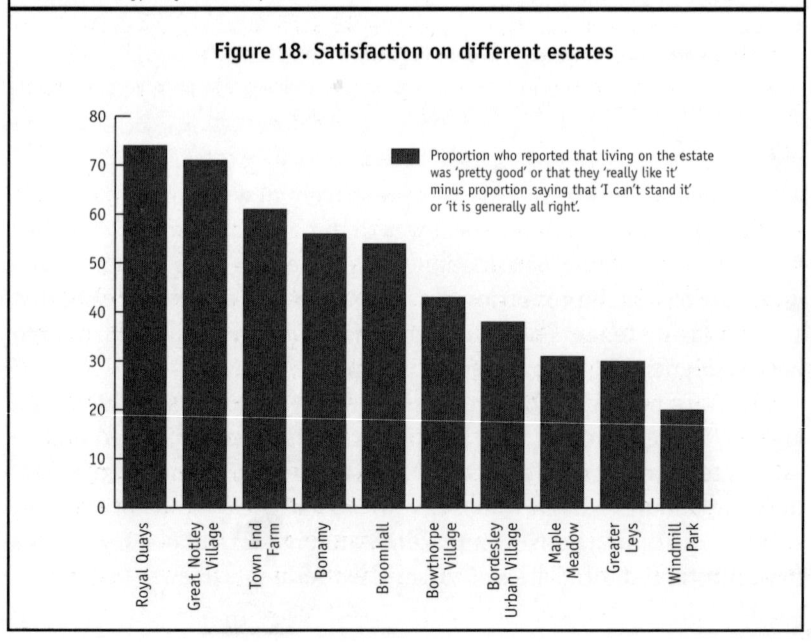

Tenure mix, problems and satisfaction

Considering these slightly lower than average results and the particularly low scores of some of our estates it is important to consider whether the mixed nature of the estates is perceived as causing dissatisfaction.

Overall impact

The overall picture from our survey is that problems and benefits associated with mixing only appear to have a slight impact on residents' satisfaction. As Figure 19 shows, the general response to mixing tenures is agnosticism. Fifty-six per cent of respondents did not think that the mixed nature of the estate created either problems or benefits. Three per cent thought that it brought both benefits and problems, 22 per cent thought that it just brought problems and 19 per cent benefits but no problems.

Figure 19. Perceptions of benefits and problems

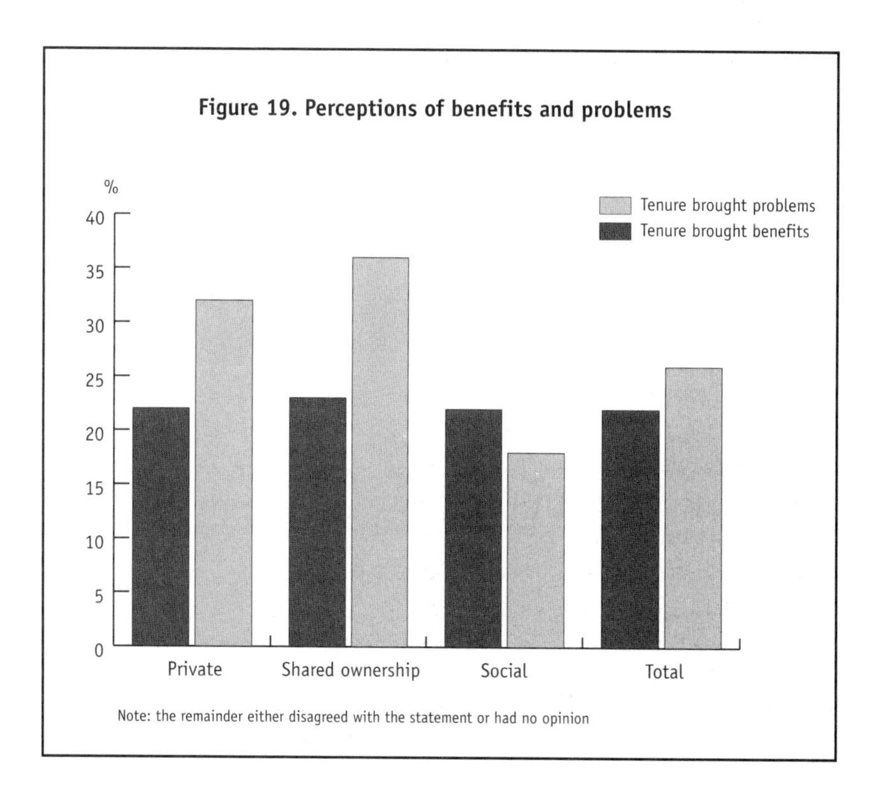

Note: the remainder either disagreed with the statement or had no opinion

Even among people who do not like living on the estate, less than half think that mixing has caused problems.[57] Conversely, residents who think that mixing brings problems can really like living on the estate. Of the quarter of respondents who thought that mixing has caused problems, more than half said that, overall, they thought that living on the estate was 'pretty good' or that they 'really liked it'. The key message, therefore, is that mixing is usually perceived to be a secondary issue. To our key question (in chapter three): 'whether tensions tend to develop between different tenure groups and, if so, how these tensions can be avoided?', the answer is that mixing does not usually cause or influence perceived problems. Other factors such as the quality of the environment, perceived safety, privacy and the friendliness of the estate are more important determinants of overall satisfaction. Overall, people who are dissatisfied are somewhat more

Figure 20. correlations between specific factors and overall feelings about living on the estate* (degree of correlation)

Perceived friendliness (0.4)
Perceived security (0.39)
Perceived privacy (0.37)
Perceived management (0.37)
Perceived noise (0.36)
Perceived architecture (0.34)
Perceived cleanliness (0.31)
Perceived graffiti/vandalism (0.28)
Perceived maintenance (0.27)
Perceived greenery (0.25)
Perceived transport and accessibility (0.16)
Frequency of using pub/cafe (0.15)
Number of people know by name (0.13)
Proportion of socialising with other estate residents (0.13)
Frequency of using community centre (0.12)

Feeling about whether mixing caused problems were not significantly correlated with overall feelings about living on the estate

* Note that these associations do not indicate which factors influences which, if any. For example, if people like the estate in general they may say that think it is friendly, irrespective of how many friends they actually have. As the table shows, that is much lower.

likely to perceive problems with mixing, but even among that group a majority think that it caused no problems. Tellingly, owners are most worried about mixing, and also tend to be most satisfied.

The exceptions

Yet like most general findings from surveys, exceptions exist to thegeneral agnosticism towards mixing and its place as a secondary issue.

As Figure 21 indicates, in a few estates, or parts of estates, a substantial minority of respondents thought that mixing had brought problems and very few thought that it had brought benefits. And even though the problems that most of those people perceive mixing to bring are minor, a few of the residents we spoke to had very strong feelings about the issue. Rare but worrying comments were made such as:

> 'we get the dregs of society moving into housing association properties. They are only after a quick pound.' (owner on tenants)

As housing managers and developers seek to minimise these, a few general lessons are important to consider.

Figure 21. Problems and benefits on different estates

Estate (ranked)	% thinking that mixing brought benefits	% thinking that mixing brought problems	Net score
1. Town End Farm	41	19	+ 21
2. Broomhall	39	21	+ 18
3. Bonamy	21	11	+ 10
4. Bowthorpe	24	20	+ 4
5. Royal Quay	28	26	+ 2
6. Greater Leys	18	18	0
7.Bordesley Village	11	26	-15
8. Windmill Park	18	40	- 22
9. Great Notley	13	37	- 24
10. Maple Meadow	5	41	- 36

1. Initial tolerance for sharing estates or streets with people from different tenures is higher than sometimes expected. But developers should still let people moving to an area know that it is mixed.

One study of mixed estates in West London suggests that owners would rather live just with other owners.[58] Our survey asked people whether they thought that owners and tenants on the estate would rather not live near those who rent. Forty-three per cent agreed, 35 per cent disagreed and 20 per cent had no opinion. That varied little among different tenure groups. It suggests that a significant minority of owners show signs of uneasiness with mix, but that intolerance is not perceived to be enormous. Of those who agreed with the statement, only about a quarter agreed with it strongly. Often those who agreed would make comments such as, 'I think that one or two do'.

The biggest association with intolerance was whether genuine problems had been identified on the estates. However, it appears that the expectations which residents come with also have some role in determining the extent to which they identify problems and hold general resentment about living in a mixed area. It was telling that those who

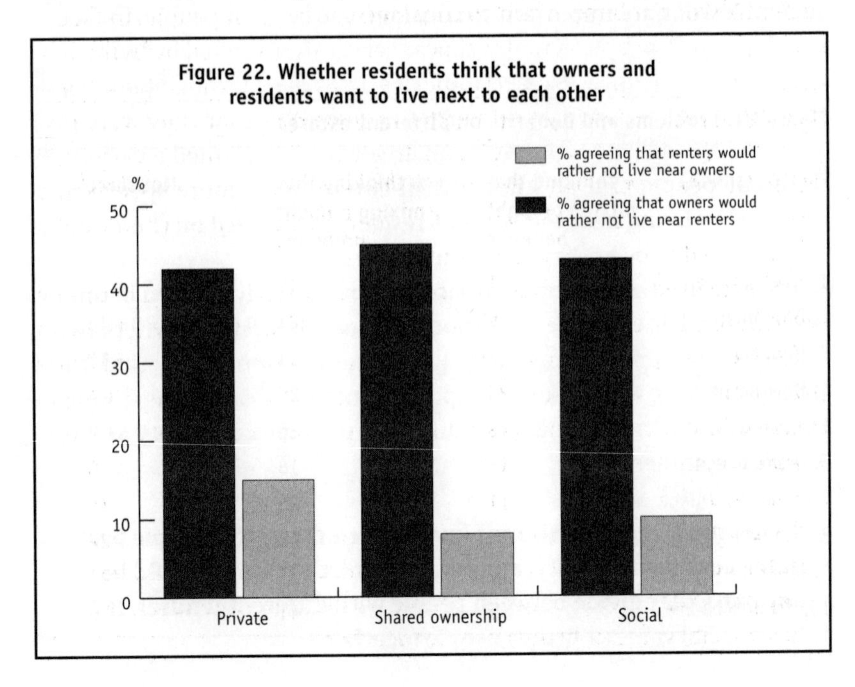

Figure 22. Whether residents think that owners and residents want to live next to each other

had moved to the estate from nearby tended to identify less problems than those who had moved from a long distance. They may have known more about the estate before arriving and therefore had more realistic expectations. Not telling owners about the mixed nature of the estate certainly appears to sometimes cause problems. For example, we heard a number of comments on estates in which prospective residents had not been informed, causing strong resentment:

> 'I was told when I bought my house that the estate was solely owner occupiers, but the surrounding properties were sold to council/housing association renters. If I had known I would not have bought the property.' (owner)

These suggest that all prospective residents should be told that the estate is mixed.

House builders may be fearful that telling owners will lower house prices. We believe that as the 'agnostic' feelings of most existing residents spreads to the general population as more mixed estates are built, then mix will not be seen as a particular issue by most people. In fact, a small group of people actually appear relatively attracted by living in a mixed area. As Figure 23 (over) indicates, in a free question about benefits, about one in twenty said without prompting that they were just attracted by the idea of living in an area which contained a variety of different people and another one in twenty were more specifically attracted by living near the types of residents who lived on their estate. These tended to be both owners and renters.

The perceived attraction to mixing was particularly marked in one or two estates. For example, in Broomhall, nearly half of owners (who tended to be quite young with high qualifications) said that they thought mixing was a good idea, predominantly because they thought that it would increase understanding and tolerance in society at large. A typical comment was

> It's [mixing] a positive thing. I know the council want people back in the centre [of the city] and I don't think that there should be any particular divide between people with different tenures. It has a social value, it brings people together.

Figure 23. Benefits of living in a mixed tenure development

Attraction	Proportion of respondents mentioning attraction
Better physical environment than estates of completely social housing, in particular because owners are perceived to keep their houses smarter, and occasionally because owners are perceived to 'keep the council on its toes'	5.5%
Attracted by the general idea of different people living in the same area, and in particular hoping that it will break down class barriers, create tolerance, etc.	5%
More specifically like the range of other residents, occasionally including the community spirit	4%
Increases aspirations, sets a good example	1%
Improves the image of an area	1%
Fewer problem families	0.5%
Other – eg better shops, practical help, shared ownership acts as a way up the housing ladder	0.5%

Note: figures rounded to the nearest 0.5%; these responses have been collated from asking respondents to note any benefits which mix brings, without prompting. These responses have been grouped into the general categories in the table. Other distinct factors were mentioned by less than 5 people (0.5% of the sample). Respondents could note as many issues as they wanted, but tended to mention just one or two.

2. When problems do occur they tend to focus around children, a few families or local issues, as is usual on estates, but on mixed estates this can cause wider resentment against mixing and particular tenure groups

Figure 24 shows the factors that residents were concerned about when they highlighted specific problems.

The factors that people mentioned were predominantly problems which tend to be raised in relation to most housing estates – vandalism, children, noise and the like. Even among the minority who complain, some identify the problems with just a few families rather than tenure groups. Comments from owners such as the one below recognise that many of those in social housing suffer equally.

> 'there's a lot of rough people who have been moved into this area who let their children run wild setting things on fire, so the oth-

Figure 24. Specific problems mentioned

Problem	Proportion of respondents mentioning problem
Crime, vandalism, anti-social behaviour	4%
Children	4%
Poor environment, particularly renters don't look after the environment and houses	3%
Snobbishness, particularly resentment from owners	2.5%
General tensions between groups/ unfriendly	2%
Problem families	1.5%
Noise	1%
Jealousy	1%
House prices	1%
Estate image	0.5%

Note: figures rounded to the nearest 0.5%; these responses have been collated from asking respondents to note any problems which mix causes, without prompting. These responses have been grouped into the general categories in the table. Other distinct factors were mentioned by less than 5 people (0.5% of the sample). Respondents could note as many issues as they wanted, but tended to mention just one or two.

> ers, *not just owner occupiers*, are losing out with the area going down from what it was when we first came. We get lorries and diggers parked outside our houses and children out all hours and muggings in the park' (emphasis added)

Yet as Figure 24 shows, a few dozen respondents – about 5 per cent of our entire sample – identified broader tensions and feelings of resentment and jealousy. In particular, on a few estates some social renters felt that owners tended not to understand or respect them. For example, about a quarter of the tenants we spoke to in Great Notley Village specifically raised such concerns without prompting. Typical comments were:

> 'Because we rent they feel we're not going to look after the properties. A lot of privately owned houses are young couples without children who can't understand why children are out in the front part – they have no respect for children.'

The challenge of mixed tenure estates is that, although mixing is usually a second order issue, specific problems can sometimes lead to general stereotyping or sense of rejection. Most worryingly, occasionally specific problems did appear to have remained unresolved and built up to the extent that real prejudice had developed. In two or three parts of estates, a pattern of conflict which anthropologists have often noted appears to have started: some actual problems take place leading to hostility which over time picks up on small cultural differences, such as language and music, in order to justify classifying people as somehow generally inferior. In the words of two owners:

> 'What is normal to them is offensive to normal people. The music is terrible and the language is absolutely foul'.

> 'They bring them up here, I guess to try to sort of integrate them. But it's dragged others down. I don't want to be snobby but *you can tell just by looking at them*. Little Beirut they call it'. (emphasis added)

That, naturally, causes a reaction. 'They seem not to see us as human' complained one tenant about the owners. 'They don't want us here, the owners don't want us – mixing is not on', said another.

For example, tensions were relatively high on Windmill Park with more than one in ten respondents alluding to general resentment, envy, snobbishness and the like. Many owners had specific complaints about vandalism and other crime. In turn, the social tenants felt stigmatised and blamed. Tensions appeared to have risen to such a level that one or two tenants we spoke to suggested that owners brought vandalism upon themselves. The private health club on the estate, named the Jealous Club, had unfortunately become a rather apt metaphor for the general souring of estate relations.

Such conflict is difficult to diffuse once it has developed to such a stage of general prejudice. Housing managers have to start tackling the prejudice as well as the specific problems.

These problems should not be over-exaggerated. They were nothing like the norm for mixed estates. Some disagreements over specific issues is also part of the process of people working out how to live together. But because tenure can become a simple marker around which resentment can become embedded – as race, age or a host of other factors can – particular care is maybe needed to avoid the problems in the first place.

3. The route to solving these isolated areas of tension is through local mediation and management, rarely from physical design. If anything, separation of different tenure groups can make it harder to reduce problems.

The physical layout of housing estates is often identified as adding to problems of estates. Interestingly, both separation and integration are sometimes blamed in mixed tenure estates. For example, one interviewee complained that clear separation induces resentment:

> 'the mixing has been done in a naïve way – all the owner occupiers are together in three blocks ... a target for abuse. Two neighbours have moved away since they were targets of abuse and a burglary.'

In contrast, one housing officer saw proximity as a problem:

> 'When owners live on the same street as renters there are generally more neighbourly disputes, especially across tenures.'

In general, house builders and housing managers tend to be most worried that street level integration will lead to disputes between neighbours. Our survey suggests that, although some residents thought that owners would rather live away from tenants, it is wrong to conclude that integration creates more problems. We found no overall correlation between degrees of segregation of the tenure types and residents actually perceiving problems with mixing tenures. For example, respondents from Maple Meadow cited greatest problems. But although shared owners and full owners had different levels of proximity (the owners separated by a wall) they were equally concerned about the mix. The estate rated second highest for problems was Windmill Park with nearly three-quarters of owners citing problems, even though they are almost completely separated from the social housing. Despite their separation, some owners still feel that their environment suffers and that children come to their part of the estate and cause problems, and some tenants still feel looked down upon. The estate which recorded the third highest complaints, Great Notley, has one of the most integrated physical designs.

We should not, therefore, think that certain styles of development are more prone to problems. In fact, if anything, integration may be good. The owners and tenants on the three most integrated estates – Town End Farm, Royal Quays and Great Notley – were the most satisfied with their estate's level of noise, security and cleanliness of public areas, factors which can spark tensions. Overall, physical integration was significantly correlated with positive feelings about living on the estate.[59] Because, as we saw in chapter four, neighbours on streets tend to have some social contact while people from different parts of the estates do not, disputes may also be slightly easier to resolve at a street level. And specific trouble makers can be more easily identified rather than broad stereotypes developing.

Integration may be working partly because it is supported by good management in itself rather than because it is helpful. And those who moved to integrated streets may be more tolerant of problems in the first place. But on the basis of our findings we believe that concern about 'pepper potting' is largely misplaced.

Nor did standard demographic characteristics of residents appear to have a significant impact on the extent to which residents saw mixing to cause problems. For example, the age, sex and ethnic origin of respondents did not appear to have an impact on perceived problems. Nor did the average income difference between different tenure groups.

Nor was social interaction associated with reduced perceptions of problems, although it can increase perceived benefits of mixed tenure developments. It does not appear that simply because people know a few people of another tenure that their concerns about mix are increased or decreased. Likewise, knowing or helping residents of another tenure was not significantly associated with whether respondents perceived that owners and renters wanted to live apart or not.

Instead, the key to reducing tensions on mixed tenure estates, as with other estates, lies in a series of management approaches. At the root of most successful estate management is good management of individual

Figure 25. The relationship between cross tenure social contact and reported problems with mixing

Number of residents known from other tenures	Noted problems	Noted benefits
None	25	18
At least one	28	29
At least five	26	38

properties and tenancies: maintenance, making sure that arrears do not build up, making sure that tenants get housing benefits they are entitled to and the like.

We did not probe the impact of property and tenancy management. But a few aspects of good management of the shared physical and social environments are highlighted by the experience of our estates.

Firstly, the importance of keeping the estate environment well maintained is emphasised. Top of the problems and benefits which mixing was perceived to bring was the impact on the physical environment. It is our experience that if the environment is well maintained people think that mixing is a good idea, their general tolerance for living with other groups remains high and tensions do not develop.

Secondly, the way in which tenure can become a badge for resentment reinforces the importance of dealing with a few families who cause particular problems. For example, local police had dealt with over 100 recorded incidents on one road of social housing over the previous eighteen months (according to their records). The owners in surrounding roads were very aware of the extent of police involvement in the social housing zone and reports of rising crime. What they were not aware of – because they live on different streets – is that only two households were responsible for practically all of the problems. So a broader cycle of mistrust has been generated between tenures on the basis of very few residents.

Thirdly, our findings of very low social interaction across estates in general and between owners and tenants in particular warns us against relying on 'the community' to establish norms of behaviour. Occasionally it is suggested that common expectations of residents behaviour – for example in relation to children's play, levels of noise, use of the street and drives, and the upkeep of gardens – develop on an estate merely by virtue of residents' shared proximity. A few residents made comments such as 'owners keep their homes tidier and it encourages us renters to keep up with them'. But most sociological research suggests that it is membership of a strong community that influences people's behaviour, not just proximity.[60] Given that such strong communities are not typical features of new housing developments, we are sceptical that common codes of behaviour will develop across them or that residents will feel much compunction about going against norms.

Our findings therefore lend weight to the need for official bodies to codify expected behaviour around issues such as noise, children and up-keep. Writing expectations into leases and tenancy agreements are definitely features of estate management that will remain important and quite probably rise in importance.

In the absence of a strong community, people in official or semi-official roles are also needed to enforce these expectations of behaviour. Again, it is unlikely that social contacts alone will provide that pressure. Nor will a few recognised senior 'members of the community' develop who have particular authority that will be respected by most people on the estate. As one housing manager noted, residents associations may have a role:

> 'Much of these [estate] problems have been averted by the strong residents association that has been operating from the beginning – forcing the tenants to take care of their gardens and the aesthetics of the estate at the same time as we ensure that we take care of the houses that are our responsibility.'

But in many areas residents associations just do not have the strength or legitimacy to mount campaigns, let alone regulate behaviour. In general our findings are therefore supportive of initiatives such as neighbourhood wardens and others who combine some official authority and a closeness to residents. These workers are likely to be drawn from outside the estate and employed by local authorities but work closely with estate residents and focus their work on the local area. They replicate some of the roles of monitoring of behaviour that close networks of contact provide in strong communities and their presence should be a deterrent from breaking expectations, as informal community leaders where they exist. In different estates the role of wardens would need to vary. In most mixed estates we have studied they would have few serious problems to deal with but their presence would probably reassure residents who know little about the others who live on the estate and would have some deterrent role. They might also have some estate overseeing role such as reporting problems with the state of the environment, public transport and the like.

Fourthly, these codes of expected or acceptable behaviour need to be established equitably and be recognised as such. Because owners are possibly more mobile and tenants seen as more likely to be 'problem' families, much of the discussion of estate management can be about managing tenants. But as the quotes in the previous section demonstrate, some tenants genuinely feel that owners look down on them and do not understand their situation. They complain that owners have unrealistic demands about, for example, stopping children playing in the road. Most owners and tenants have very similar aspirations, but in order to avoid a sense of injustice and to provide genuine equal rights, any codes of behaviour should be estate-wide (covering owners and tenants equally) and transparently developed in consultation with all residents.

Conclusions

Most of estates we have studied are doing reasonably well. They certainly seem to be avoiding the downward cycle of environmental, economic and social problems characteristic of the 'worst estates' which are the focus of government policy. None had serious problems with letting, although one or two had problems with high turnover. Most had rising property prices.

On average, residents held slightly less positive views about their estates than did respondents to our national survey of the British population. But that does not generally appear to arise from their mixed nature, at least in the views of residents. No significant correlation exists between residents' overall feelings about living on the estate and whether they perceive mixing to cause problems. Rather, the slightly less positive views are more likely to be explained by the relative neediness of social housing residents, lower than average incomes of owners and relative young age of residents.

In general, residents are agnostic about living on a mixed estate. About a quarter see benefits, a quarter problems and just over half neither problems or benefits. Over time we believe that these perceptions will spread to the population as whole. It is important to stress that mixing tenures at the level of the street does not appear to create greater problems or tensions. Residents of 'pepper-potted' schemes are certainly no more likely to report problems with mixing. And residents of estates with considerable road mixing actually rated their estates more highly overall and for specific issues such a security and vandalism than more segregated estates. We therefore suggest that mixing tenures at road level is often preferable to separating them into different roads or zones.

Unfortunately, in a few circumstances, tenure differences can compound problems. If general problems occur on an estate, even if just focused on one or two families, owners can develop prejudices about tenants in general. Tenants, in turn, feel looked down upon. At best, that can hinder a sense of co-operation and in a very few circumstances can be used as an excuse by some tenants to have less consideration for the property and privacy of owners. Once prejudice and resentment develop they can require particular efforts to defuse. The need to avoid such resentment creates, therefore, further impetus to keep problems of vandalism, noise and children causing a nuisance to a minimum.

Finally, given the weakness of community in general and cross-tenure contact in particular on mixed tenure estates, we have to recognise the role of officials or semi-officials in creating trust, being a recognisable face and identifiable presence, monitoring problems, helping establish fair and mutually understood expectations of behaviour and being a first contact to help, intervene or mediate in disputes between residents. Close communities with dense networks of contacts and recognised leaders often solve disputes and develop co-operation without external help, but in the absence of such communities on most mixed and non-mixed estates, people such as neighbourhood wardens need to take them on.

6. Conclusion

A comprehensive analysis of the costs and benefits of mixed tenure developments must wait until research is also completed into their impact on local economies, estate image, public services and estate management.[61] This research into social relations does, however, allow us to draw some conclusions which should help policy-makers develop more appropriate expectations for mixed estates and improve their design and management. Six stand out.

1. The most important finding is probably that the mixed or unmixed nature of the estate is usually only a minor or non-existent issue for most residents, owners and tenants. More than half of residents of mixed tenure estates perceive no problems or benefits arising from mix; they are agnostic. And where problems are perceived, they tend only to have a small influence people's overall perception of the estate: no significant correlation existed between residents' overall feelings about the estate and their perceptions of whether mix causes problems or not. Conversely, when benefits are perceived they are often fairly vague, such as a general belief that it is good for people from all backgrounds to live together. Only about one in ten respondents to our survey mentioned more specific benefits such as creating a good physical environment or attracting shops.

   Critics and champions of mixed tenure schemes should note that agnosticism. The fears of some housing professionals that mixing is very unpopular with residents appear largely unfounded. Often these fears are based on a few anecdotes. Our wider survey suggest that they are not representative of most resident's experiences. Problems are localised and rare. Proponents of mix should also be cautious. While residents of areas once dominated by large council estates – Bonamy, Broomhall and Town End Farm – are relatively positive about having a mix, even these people usually perceive the influence to be limited. Mixing may help an area avoid decline in the long term, but few residents notice the day-to-day impact.

2. Integrating tenures within streets – rather than segregating the tenures into different streets – is generally endorsed by our findings. Residents of estates, or parts of estates, with considerable integration within streets reported no greater perceived problems with mixing than those of zoned estates. They were also significantly more positive about the estates overall. Having only considered ten estates, these findings must be treated with a little caution. But our general view is that with a slightly careful allocations policy and some broad shared rules and expectations (for example about children) mixing at the street level is unlikely to lead to tensions in all but the rarest of circumstances and can create a better environment. And given that street level mixing also helps reduce the chance that certain streets will develop a bad image because they are perceived to be all social houses – such labelling certainly occurs – we believe that street level mixing is preferable to putting different tenures in different zones. Very few developers, housing associations or local authorities currently pursue such a street level approach. Instead, they separate tenures into different streets or zones. Our findings should make them reconsider that policy.

3. While problems are rare, if specific problems do occur, tenure can sometimes become a factor that divides residents. Slightly fewer than one in twenty of our respondents mentioned general tensions developing between tenures. These usually started with specific issues, such as children or a few families who cause disruption. But when tenants get blamed in general, as they sometimes do, a broader pattern of resentment can draw in a significant minority of owners and tenants. That reinforces the need to avoid or rectify problems in the first place.

4. While developers and housing managers should not fear that the mixed nature of estates is likely to make them unpopular or lead to tensions, social policy analysts should also be careful about making claims for a new sort of community on such estates. On many of the estates labelled 'mixed tenure', tenures are separated into different streets. On such estates, only a small minority of residents are likely to know residents of any other tenure, at least for the first ten years or so. That lack of contact may be in small part due to the different interests of residents and owners and, occasionally, prejudice. But in the main, low contact between owners and renters simply reflects generally low social contact between residents of different streets. Predominantly, people only know their closest neighbours, even on large estates. It is therefore difficult to see the practical social network benefits for the majority of those living in the types of mixed tenure estates which are typically built today. They are unlikely to share resources, knowledge about the labour market, come into contact with role models or develop greater tolerance because they are unlikely to meet people from different economic groups.

   With street level mixing, very significantly higher cross-tenure contact develops. Probably more than half of residents will know the name of at least one resident with a different tenure. A smaller proportion could ask for help or advice. That is another reason why street level mixing is, in our view, preferable to the usual practice of zoning estates into private and social housing sections. But even with street level mixing policy-makers should be realistic: these levels of social interaction between different economic groups in the relatively new mixed roads which we studied are hardly sufficient to create a considerably more inclusive society. If such societies ever develop, the process will take a long time.

5. Fostering greater estate-wide contact without street level mixing is likely to be an uphill struggle. Most British do not think that they share many common interests with those who live locally. And our findings suggest that they tend not to meet other residents in public spaces such as parks, pubs or local shops. Fostering social networks that span estates requires more active and facilitated

measures, for example around a community centre, rather than simply building public amenities. But even the most successful community centres tend only to attract a minority of residents.

The best hope for fostering estate-wide communities is to increase the length of time people live in houses (which may have other drawbacks such as requiring people to commute further) or to develop better local mechanisms for sharing information and resources, for example through local web pages and newsletters, so that people are aware of their common interests.

6. Such lack of close community may make it slightly harder for people to come together to tackle common problems, but in no way impossible. Many people are fairly used to working with others who they do not know very well. Given the right structures and a sense of local belonging, residents will often get together to tackle common problems such as poor maintenance or a particular rise in crime on a one-off basis. Those structures may be, for example, a small neighbourhood group or individual who acts as focal point for others if serious problems develop. The presence of these groups or individuals may be as important to an area's 'social capital' as the number of group members or extent of informal networks. They are the lightening conductors for collective action.

Our main message is, therefore, fairly simple:

- today's new mixed tenure developments are unlikely to have an enormous impact on people's lives or create a very inclusive community, but most appear to have avoided a downward spiral into deprivation, and
- in the future mixing at street level should often be pursued in preference to confining different tenures to different roads.

The findings also add to our understanding of local communities on fairly new housing estates in general, for the nature of social relations on mixed estates is probably fairly similar to that found on most estates.

Local communities have long been perceived as more of a feature of the past than the present. Nineteenth century writers struggled to come to terms with the rapid displacement of members of traditional rural communities into the rapidly expanding cities of Britain. Wordsworth wrote about cities as places in which people did not even know their neighbours. By the second half of the twentieth century it was the suburbs that were the chief villains in killing community. Lewis Mumford's famous 1961 chronicle *The History of the City*, laments that

> '[the suburban] movement from the centre carries no hope or promise of life at a higher level. Just as our expanding technological universe pushes our daily existence ever further from its human centre, so the expanding urban universe carries its separate fragments ever farther from the city, leaving the individual more dissociated, lonely and helpless than he probably was ever before.'[62]

The extent to which local communities were ever the all-embracing social entity which nostalgia credits them with is uncertain. Nor has locality ceased to have any social relevance for people. But we do not believe that strong local communities involving most residents are likely to develop on most new developments. People know a few others, mainly on their street, but their main social and work activities do not revolve around their neighbourhood. One sociologist estimates that North Americans know on average 1,000 to 2,000 others but that only ten to twenty of these are local.[63]

Further, most people seem to feel relatively happy about that. One recent report found that out of a long list of possible factors which could make 'somewhere a good place to live', having family and friends living nearby was second from last. It was mentioned by just one in five respondents.[64] People can often rely on a wide network of friends and acquaintances beyond their immediate neighbourhood for help and advice. Better transport and communications, higher female workforce participation, more leisure time and general increases in geographical mobility all contribute to the expansion of these diverse networks. Consequently, if the government wants to help improve people's social lives and informal mutual support networks, it would often do better supporting people's diverse contacts through better transport and communications than focusing on local societies. It tends to be specific groups such as mothers with young children, young people and the elderly who particularly rely on local contacts.

Trying to create strong local communities – mixed or not - might, therefore, never a particularly realistic policy goal. Further, we may not want to create them. Strong communities also often have negative attributes such as unjust hierarchies, insularity and prejudice against strangers. Instead, the local policy agenda is to look for new ways to reproduce some of the beneficial attributes of strong local communities in an environment of relatively diverse and weak local social ties. These attributes include:

- collective action
- pressure against anti-social behaviour
- trust in other local people.

Collective action. Although probably easier within a strong local community, we believe that some collective action to improve a neighbourhood or street is possible even without one. On many of the estates we studied, people got together when they really needed to and went their separate ways when issues diminished in importance. We believe that the key to allowing such co-operation to develop quickly is to have a small local group or even individuals who can become focal points if issues arise. A second factor is probably some sense of local belonging. Supporting local 'social capital' is as much about maintaining these as it is supporting 'community' in general. That might be, for example, by providing such groups or people with easy access to information about the plans of the local authority, housing association, police and other agencies; bringing local problems to their attention; providing them with meeting rooms or computer facilities if they need them; ensuring that a community development worker stays in occasional contact with them, helps them get in contact with a network of such activists and quickly responds to important issues which they raise.

Abiding by shared values and creating trust are features of close communities that loose networks rarely reproduce to the same extent. That is because people do not, as it were, all belong to the same 'club' where they all know each other and feel a sense of membership. This lack of self-regulation among loose networks does not, however, mean that the only options for reducing anti-social behaviour on estates is to encourage homogenous communities or extend the law and number of policemen. Rather, a combination of explicit expectations for everyone living on an estate and more workers with roles such as neighbourhood wardens could well make a considerable difference. The people who are needed are those who combine authority with a very detailed knowledge of an area and its residents. Like traditional community leaders they need to be rooted in a locality and recognisable by all. Unlike traditional community leaders they must derive their authority from the local council, residents association and public agencies rather than informal hierarchies.

The presence of such wardens and other neighbourhood workers should in itself increase people's sense of security and help prevent problems. So an environment can be created in which people trust others to act reasonably even if they have little personal contact with each other. Local agreements about anti-social behaviour, the use of public space and the like can also help create such trust. The challenge is to develop these agreements and wardens in co-operation with all the residents rather than impose them in a way which makes some residents feel victimised.

Appendix 1. The Estates

The estates below are ranked in order of the degree of social contact the survey recorded between residents with different tenures. That was based on a composite measure of the number of residents of a different tenure that respondents knew and helped. In some of the estates, only parts of the estates were surveyed (indicated below). The rank should not, therefore, be treated as necessarily indicative of interaction on the estate as a whole.

1. Town End Farm

Town End Farm estate was built in the early 1960s on the edge of Sunderland and forms part of a large swathe of local authority accommodation built to re-house residents from run down inner city and shipbuilding neighbourhoods. But by the late 1980s the estate was itself described by the Government as having 'some of the worse housing stock in the country.' At the turn of the 1990s, the council started a major renovation of the estate.

Diversifying the tenure was one of the objectives of the re-development. In particular, single flats had become difficult to let. The council stock was reduced from 1,332 houses and 988 flats to 1,020 houses and 90 flats. The remainder were demolished or sold to a major house builder and a housing association. In particular, small blocks of flats that were dispersed throughout the estate were converted into private housing (assisted with a grant). The remaining council stock was significantly improved internally and externally with a variety of grants.

The estate also fell within a City Challenge area, which provided money to redevelop a shopping parade and support a policing task force and training opportunities.

We surveyed residents across the estate, but concentrated around the clusters of new private housing. The people who we surveyed appeared to have particularly high social contact with those of other tenures for a number of reasons. The most important reason is probably the physical proximity between the tenures. Given that most private housing is in blocks of just four houses, it would be difficult for owners to know many neighbours without knowing tenants. The economic profile of people living in the two types of tenure is probably also an important factor in the high level of contact. The estate had the second most equal income distribution between the tenure groups. That is probably unsurprising given the fact that the private houses could be bought for about £40,000 when first built. In other words, tenure is less of a proxy for economic background on Town End Farm than in estates where the private housing costs many tens or hundreds of thousands of pounds. Residents also told us that quite a few of the people who bought houses were already from the estate or had some link with the estate. When the new private houses were first built the estate had such a bad external reputation, and is in a fairly inaccessible area, that it tended to be people with an existing link who bought.

2. Greater Leys

Greater Leys is an extension to the large Blackbird Leys estate on the edge of Oxford. Blackbird Leys was built in the 1960s. It is close to the Cowley car factory and mainly comprises local authority dwellings. Greater Leys is a recent extension to the estate on 124 acres to the south of the original development. Nearly 2,000 properties have been built since the scheme started in 1990, of which 54 per cent are rented from housing associations, 17 per cent are being partly bought under shared ownership arrangements and 29 per cent were sold outright. According to one report it is currently the largest new build social housing development in the country.[65]

The primary aim of the development was to provide new social housing. In the words of the chair of Oxford City Council Housing Committee, 'the council remains committed to the provision of good standard affordable homes for local people'.[66] Land was sold off for private housing in order to fund community services and infrastructure. The rented, shared ownership and private housing is broadly laid out in three zones, progressively further from the link road with the original Blackbird Leys development. A new ring road gives access to the development without driving through the old estate. The private housing tends to be 're-badged' as small developments such as 'Oxford Village' although some roads contain a mixed of tenures, usually either shared ownership and private housing or shared ownership and social rented housing. We primarily studied the streets which had a mixture.

The development has been supported with considerable investment in the social infrastructure: community facilities, youth clubs, a centre for the elderly, a park, six play areas, funding for a bus route, and training and employment opportunities for disabled and young people.

The relatively high interaction is probably due to the geographical proximity of the shared ownership and other tenures. Most of the mixing took place between shared owners and social tenants. Over a third of social housing tenants knew someone with a shared ownership arrangement. About seven out of ten shared owners knew somebody who rented from a housing association. The interaction between the outright owners and other tenures was very low, lower than on estates such as Bowthorpe or Broomhall. The place of shared owners as the focus of cross-tenure interaction supports the idea that small income differences between tenure groups increases the likelihood of contact between the residents.

3. Bowthorpe Village, Norwich

Bowthorpe village is a large development on the eastern edge of Norwich. The area was bought by the city council in the early 1970s, but building only got going in the late 1970s. So far, approximately 2,300 houses have been built on the 254 acre site, along with a shopping centre, an industrial and retail area, schools and other community facilities. New houses are still being built. The estate is adjacent to other local authority estates on one side and open countryside on the other. It is in a relatively deprived part of the city. The idea of Bowthorpe was to create a relatively self contained area – it still only has one access road. It has its own shops (although the supermarket has just closed), a number of youth and community projects, a church and a neighbourhood police station.

We mainly studied an older part of the development called Clover Hill. It was planned as a distinct 'hamlet' of about 1,600 properties, with its own pub, community hall and one or two shops. Overall, the aim is to create a equal number of private and social houses in Bowthorpe. But Clover Hill has about 60 per cent social housing. Roads tend to be of the same tenure, but we did include one or two roads which contain a mixture of tenures.

Much of the higher than average interaction can be put down to the length of time that residents had lived in the area. Secondly, because it is a large area, users of the schools, shops, pubs and clubs are mainly residents from Bowthorpe. With a mixture of tenures across the estate these user groups are likely to be fairly mixed as well. We found, for example, that those people who used the supermarket regularly (the survey was undertaken before it shut) were more likely to know people of other tenures.

4. Great Notley Village

Great Notley Village is a new greenfield development just outside Braintree, north Essex. It aims to become a new 'garden village': 2,000 homes with shops, village hall, primary school, church, country park, pub and other leisure facilities dispersed over 465 acres. To date about a 1,000 properties (approximately half the housing) have been built.

Negotiations over the development of the site started in the mid-1980s and building in 1993. The eventual planning consent depended on providing a number of benefits to the local community, including building 50 social housing units for free, which have been given to the local housing association on the condition that the local authority can nominate all the tenants. These have been supplemented by another 100 properties which the housing association bought from the developer.

The social renting houses have been clustered in small bunches (six to ten houses) and are architecturally identical to the private housing. A few have been bought under shared ownership arrangements. Our survey focused on the area in which much of the social housing is found. It was also one of the first areas built.

Although the social housing tenants and owners have pretty different economic circumstances, it appears that the shear physical proximity has led to above average contact. In particular, most of those we interviewed in social housing knew some owners. Given their small numbers it would be difficult for them only to know other social tenants. The community centre may also have played a role. A relatively large proportion of respondents from both tenures used it. The shops focus around a large supermarket. But we did not find any association between the frequency of use and levels of social contact with residents of other tenures.

5. Royal Quays

Royal Quays, a development of about 1,000 homes, lies on the north shore of the Tyne, between Newcastle and the coast. The site was once an industrial area and a dock, but during the 1980s had suffered considerable economic decline. The adjacent Meadowhall estate suffered from severe deprivation and a reputation for social problems.

In redeveloping the wider area, one of the primary aims of the Tyne and Wear Development Corporation was 'reviving the riverside areas as a place to live: including developing mixed communities with affordable homes for rent and purchase ... [and] to ensure that regeneration benefits the whole community: by ensuring that at least 25 per cent of housing development is social housing.'[67] Royal Quays was the flagship development in that plan. About 40 per cent of the properties built so far are social housing, including a small number of shared ownership properties. The area that we studied – in which the houses were built in 1993 and 1994 – contains a mix of housing on most streets.

The housing has been supported by considerable investment in the social, economic and environmental infrastructure: a community centre, a nearby retail and leisure centre, a large new Twinings Tea factory and parks. The area is also covered by the North Tyneside City Challenge, which has invested in the general social infrastructure of North Shields and the surrounding estates.

Although the physical integration appears important, integration also appeared enhanced by a more genuine sense of collective belonging to the estate than existed on most of the estates we studied. One person with close involvement with the community centre probably exaggerates the case, but her views found some resonance in the interviews we carried out with a spectrum of the population:

> 'Walking down the street, you would not know the difference between an owner and a renter, even if you spoke to them'.
>
> *Questioner:* 'Is that because houses cost less to buy here?'
>
> 'No, I think it is just because people don't have that prejudice about being a renter or an owner. On the residents association we have a similarly mixed participation of all the tenures. People are very close in this community. We also have some successful professionals on the estate – we have chief executives of local authorities and people high up in the universities.'

Many residents talked about the estate as developing something approaching a genuinely mixed community. In much of the estate, that has been supported by a very careful policy of allocations and action against tenants causing trouble by the main housing association and the estate community centre is also more used by residents than on most estates.

6. Broomhall

Broomhall is a medium-sized development in central Sheffield. It had once been an area of council flats. These were cheaply constructed and in a poor state of repair.

At the end of the 1980s the old flats were demolished and work started on a new development, which the local authority wanted to contain a mix of tenures. The new homes were completed in 1994 and 1995; 270 properties were built, mainly flats. Of these about 170 went to two housing associations and 100 were sold privately. Some of the private houses have been rented out privately. One of the housing associations caters for ethnic minorities and, in particular, houses a large number of Somalis.

The site has more private housing on one side, more social on the other. However, the interface is quite open and the predominantly social housing area also contains a number of small clusters of private housing (rows of three or four houses and small blocks of flats). Again, we focused the survey on the more mixed parts.

The mixing was higher among the owners, suggesting that it arose primarily from the owners who are in the more pepper-potted sections of the social housing. In the zone of private flats fewer appeared to have much contact with other social tenants.

The scheme is generally seen as fairly successful, with prices of the private houses rising and the housing association reporting relatively few problems.

7. Bonamy

Bonamy is in inner south east London, a mile or two south of the river Thames, in the borough of Southwark. The new development is mainly on the site of a 950 property council estate which was built in the 1960s. The original flats had structural and technical problems, and the area suffered from vandalism and high rates of crime. It also contained a very strong local community, once based around the docks.

In 1989 the local authority, a major building firm and a housing association formed a consortium to redevelop the area. The original core of the estate was redeveloped as just over 300 local authority houses and flats in low rise blocks. On one side of the estate, 300 properties were built for housing associations (mainly houses). On the other side, separately by a fairly busy road, 180 properties were built for ownership and shared ownership. About a third of these are shared ownership, two-thirds were sold outright. Most of these are separated and have different access roads. The bulk of the social housing was completely in 1995, the private housing slightly later.

The sale of properties for outright sale helped finance the whole development, but the scheme is also presented as developing a 'mixed tenure community'.[68] A community centre has been built between the council and private housing, but the estate has few other specific amenities. Most established shops and amenities are within a mile of the estate.

The survey covered the whole of the estate. Because the different tenures are so segregated we were unable to focus on the more integrated parts as we did on many other estates. The main mixing that did occur was between those who owned and those who were shared owners. Some of that was from a couple of blocks of private housing in the shared ownership section, but some contact also appeared to take place between shared owners and owners from parts of the estate with different access roads.

8. Maple Meadow

Maple Meadow is a small development of about 150 houses on the outskirts of Plympton, near Plymouth. It is part of a large housing area that has been developed over the last decade. It is also the newest of the developments that we studied. The houses were only completed eighteen months ago.

About a quarter of the houses are private. The rest are split evenly between rented and shared ownership. The rented and shared ownership properties are on different roads, apart from one road which is mixed. Although the private properties were built at the same time and have a similar style, they have a different access road and are only connected by a path. A few private houses from a slightly older private road next to the social housing development were also sampled in order to make up the numbers.

The estate has a small play area and is close to a primary school and nursery. Otherwise, the nearest facilities are some new shops and a community centre about a half a mile away or the centre of Plympton (about one and a half miles).

The main interaction which did take place was between shared owners and social tenants. The owners appeared to generally avoid contact with the renters, partly due to physical separation but also because very low opinions of the social renters had developed among the owners.

9. Bordesley Urban Village

Bordesley claims to be the first 'urban village in Britain'. It aims to create a sense of a self-contained area with a cross-section of people. It is close to the centre of Birmingham and was originally a mixed industrial and housing area. It was severely run down with derelict land and a declining population.

The process of regenerating the area started in 1989, under the auspices of the city council and Birmingham Heartlands Ltd (later Heartlands Development Corporation). It is nearly complete. One of the major aims was to bring new housing to the area, particularly private housing for local residents. Altogether, 750 new properties have been built (about 100 for housing associations and the rest private) and 350 local authority properties refurbished. The first private housing was given a subsidy of £12,500 per property. The area now has slightly more private housing than social housing. Much of the housing has been developed as separate blocks within the overall development, and these are usually mono-tenure.

The housing development has been supported with extensive environmental improvements, such moving out polluting factories, redeveloping a park, building a small row of shops, a 'village hall' and a doctor's surgery, and also with economic and training support for local businesses.

Social contact appeared to be very low partly because the design of the housing is focused on relatively small areas that are invariably of the same tenure. But we also got the impression of an area which has yet to develop significant social interaction among the owners in general.

10. Windmill Park

Windmill Park is a new estate on the site of a former psychiatric hospital in Hanwell, in the London Borough of Ealing (west London). After the hospital closed, a consortium of housing associations and private developers redeveloped the site. The estate borders a major road into Ealing and central London in one direction, towards Heathrow airport in the other. Housing demand is very high in the area for both private and social properties.

Properties were finished between 1993 and 1996. The old hospital buildings themselves have been converted into approximately 200 private flats. In the old grounds, approximately 550 houses were built for rent by housing associations and 100 for shared ownership. The private properties are separated from the rest of the development with their own car parking facilities. The shared ownership properties are more integrated, but on different roads from the rented properties. The estate also has a range of purpose-built facilities: community centre, private nursery, grocer's shop, health club and post office.

What little contact did exist was almost exclusively between the shared owners and the social tenants. Fewer than one in ten of the owners we interviewed knew anybody from the other section of the estate.

Appendix 2. The fieldwork

In order to assess the extent of residents' social contact, in particular whether a community is developing across different tenure groups, we asked residents:

- how many people they knew by name on the estate, and how many people they knew of who lived in a property of a different tenure
- the extent to which they rely on other any residents, and in particular those with a different tenure, for help with tasks, and various types of advice:
  - DIY and gardening
  - lending and borrowing (if you needed tools, or a cup of sugar)
  - transport (for example if you wanted a lift somewhere)
  - child care and baby sitting
  - shopping (would you ask people to bring you things back from the shops)
  - problems at work
  - finding a job
  - getting help with filling in forms
  - getting advice about money
- what proportion of the time they spend on leisure activities is spent with people from the estate.

In order to attempt to explain the influences on the development of social networks on mixed tenure estates we asked residents:

- how they got to know people on the estate, including, for example, because they were brought up together, live next door or met at the local shops
- how often they use local facilities and amenities
- the role of children, such as how many people they have got to know through a school or nursery and of which tenure
- the role of work, such as how far away they work
- a characteristics of different tenure groups, such as their income, education, and age
- the role of tensions and animosity between different tenure groups.

We also considered the geographical layout of estates, the provision of community facilities and other amenities on them and some of the history of the estates.

Survey

The questionnaire was designed by Demos, with piloting in four mixed tenure estates in London.

The survey was undertaken by Demos and Public Attitude Surveys between October 1998 and February 1999. The survey was conducted face to face in people's homes or on their doorsteps. Each interview lasted between 25 and 40 minutes.

In each estate, 150 addresses were identified and houses visited up to four times until 90 completed interviews were completed (assuming a 60 per cent response rate). The sample was designed to provide a mix of tenures and hence clustered in parts of the estate. The sample areas were also biased towards the older parts of estates and those with greater mixing of tenures. In Great Notley, Maple Meadow, Bordesley and Broomhall, the initial sample just failed to provide 90 completed interviews. A few extra properties were therefore added to the survey.

In addition to the initial 90 interviews on each site, Demos staff also interviewed another ten residents to give a total of appropriately 100 interviews from each estate. These were selected to meet broad quotas of a mix of tenure, sex and age in order for Demos staff to gain maximum exposure to the range of perspectives. The questionnaire was often followed by a less structured discussion.

NOP omnibus survey

In order to better interpret residents' perceptions of mixed tenure estates, a few questions from our survey of mixed tenure residents were also placed in the NOP national omnibus survey. The questions concerned people's perception of their estate (or immediate local area if they did not live on an estate).

This omnibus survey covered 2,000 people. The responses were weighted in order to provide a representative sample of the British population. The responses from this representative sample of the British population were compared with those from our sample of 1,000 mixed tenure residents in order to assess the relative merits of mixed tenure developments.

A full copy of the questionnaire and responses for both the mixed tenure survey and omnibus survey have been deposited with the ESRC Data Archive at the University of Essex.

Respondent details

Tenure mix: 33 per cent rented from housing associations, 14 per cent rented from the local authority, 4 per cent rented privately, 38 per cent were owner occupiers, 10 per cent shared ownership and less than 1 per cent had bought their house through right to buy.

Gender: 65 per cent female, 35 per cent male. That varied from 58 per cent female in Bonamy to 73 per cent in Town End Farm.

Age: Overall, slightly younger than the population as a whole. Sixteen per cent eighteen to 24; 36 per cent 25 to 34; 28 per cent 35 to 49; 13 per cent 50 to 64; and 8 per cent over 65. The elderly tended to be in older estates: 40 per cent over 50 in Norwich, 30 per cent in Sunderland. Proportions were fairly similar between tenure groups.

Ethnic group: 82 per cent white, 8 per cent black, 5 per cent from Indian sub-continent and 5 per cent other. Considerable variation existed between estates: from 56 per cent white in Bordesley, Birmingham to 100 per cent in Town End Farm, Sunderland. Housing association residents had more ethnic minorities (28 per cent), owner occupied (15 per cent), shared owners and local authority tenants (10 per cent).

Length of residence and how far away previously lived: the estates were all built between two and fifteen years ago, with the exception of Town End Farm (Sunderland) and Bonamy (Southwark) which were redevelopments of long-established council estates. In all the estates, apart from Great Notley Village (Essex), the majority of interviewees had previously lived less than five miles away. Overall, 15 per cent had lived in their house for less than a year, 29 per cent one to two years, 40 per cent three to five years, 16 per cent over five years.

Socio-economic class: Almost national average of ABC1s (40 per cent). Fewer C2s (skilled manual) than national average (17 per cent rather than 25 per cent) and more Es (reliant on state benefits) – 24 per cent compared to 13 per cent nationally.

Working status: 37 per cent full time, 15 per cent part time, 7 per cent unemployed, 5 per cent sick or disabled, 21 per cent looking after family, 11 per cent retired.

Housing type: The vast majority are small and medium sized houses, with 32 per cent two bedroom and 46 per cent three bedroom. Only 11 per cent in flats.

Notes

1. The American Anthropological Association, 4350 North Fairfax Drive, Suite 640, Arlington Virginia.
2. For example, the Government consultation paper *Modernising Local Government: Local democracy and community leadership* (1998, Department of Environment, Transport and the Regions) emphasises the way in which local government is expected to work in partnership with local people.
3. Young M and Lemos G, 1997, *The Communities We Have Lost and Can Regain*, Lemos and Crane, London.
4. Etzioni A, 1995, *The Spirit of Community: Rights, responsibilities and the communitarian agenda*, Fontana Press, London, ix.
5. Social Exclusion Unit, 1998, *Bringing Britain Together: A national strategy for neighbourhood renewal*, Cabinet Office, London, 7.
6. For example, the Social Exclusion Unit set up eighteen Policy Action Teams to help devise and deliver policies to tackle the problems of the poorest neighbourhoods.
7. Hills J, 1998, *Income and Wealth: The latest evidence*, Joseph Rowntree Foundation, York.
8. Lee A, and Hills J, 1999, *New Cycles of Disadvantage?*, report of a conference organised by CASE on behalf of ESRC for HM Treasury, Centre For the Analysis of Social Exclusion, London School of Economics, London.
9. Social Exclusion Unit, 1998 (note 5), 17.
10. Power A and Tunstall R, 1995, *Swimming Against the Tide: Polarisation or progress on twenty unpopular council estates, 1980-1995*, Joseph Rowntree Foundation, York, 4.
11. Office for National Statistics, 1999, *UK in Figures*, ONS, London.
12. cited Lemos and Young, 1997 (notes 3).
13. Ibid.
14. Family Expenditure Survey, 1961 to 1993, excluding housing benefit, median income in 1996 prices for social renters (all population), cited Giles C, Johnson P, McCrae J, Taylor J, 1996, *Living with the State: The incomes and work incentives of tenants in the social rented sector*, Institute for Fiscal Studies, London, 45.
15. Donnison, 1994, *Act Local: Social justice from the bottom up*, IPPR, London, cited in Kintrea K, 1997, *Can Owner Occupation Regenerate Deprived Housing Estates? Propositions on socially mixed*

neighbourhoods and some empirical evidence, unpublished paper, Department of Urban Studies, University of Glasgow.

16. London Pride Partnership, 1998, *Affordable Homes in London*, London Pride Partnership, London, 32.

17. Such problems of stigmatisation of areas have been particularly emphasised by the Joseph Rowntree Foundation. For example, its director Richard Best quoted in 'Upward and mobile' (*RIBA journal* 26 March 1999) noted 'we need to develop thriving mixed communities in the inner cities ... Otherwise we risk a similar situation to the USA where better off families live in suburbs while poorer people are relegated to stigmatised inner urban areas.'

18. Goss J, 1995, 'We know who you are and we know where you live: the instrumental rationality of geo-demographic systems, *Economic Geography*, vol 71, no 2.

19. See *Guardian*, 15 September 1999, 'Mixed talent makes or breaks a school', in which it is argued that with more than 30 per cent of disturbed or disadvantaged pupils almost no teacher can succeed.

20. Power and Tunstall, 1995 (note 10), 15

21. 6 P, 1997, *Escaping Poverty: From safety nets to networks of opportunity*, Demos, London.

22. Discussed in Kintrea, 1997 (note 15).

23. Department of the Environment, Transport and the Regions, 1992, *Planning Policy Guidance Note 3*, DETR, London.

24. Department of the Environment, Transport and the Regions, 1997, *Consultation Paper: Draft circular on planning and affordable housing*, DETR, London, 1.

25. Department of the Environment, Transport and the Regions, 1999, *Revision of Planning Policy Guidance Note 3: Housing public consultation draft*, DETR, London, Paras 11-16.

26. Department of the Environment, Transport and the Regions, 1998, *Planning the Communities of the Future*, DETR, London, 23.

27. Urban Task Force, 1999, *Towards an Urban Renaissance: Final report of the Urban Task Force chaired by Lord Rogers of Riverside*, Urban Task Force, London, 49, 71.

28. London Pride Partnership, 1998 (note 16), pg 32

29. Page D, 1994, *Developing Communities*, Sutton Hastoe Housing Association, Middlesex, 6–7.

30. Dixon L, 1997, 'Love thy neighbour? Social interaction on mixed estates' paper to ENHR/YHR seminar *European Housing in Transition*, Geographical Research Institute, Hungarian Academy of Sciences, cited in Cole I and Shayer S, [unpublished paper], 'Tenure mix as social fix', Sheffield Hallam University, 8, which suggests that one-third of local authorities in England and Wales and two-thirds of the top 200 housing associations are already actively involved in developing on a multi-tenure basis; see also Lemos and Young, 1997 (note 3), 59.

31. DETR, 1998, *The Government's Response*, DETR, London, para 118.

32. Klienman M, 1998, *Include Me Out? The new politics of place and poverty*, CASE paper 11, London School of Economics, London, 2.

33. Wilson WJ, 1991, 'Studying inner-city social dislocations: the challenge of public agenda research', *American Sociological Review*, vol 56, no 1-14, 10.
34. Jargowsky, PA, 1996, *Poverty and Place: Ghettos, barrios and the American city*, Russell Sage, New York.
35. Holman, B, 1998, *Faith in the Poor*, Lion Publishing, Oxford.
36. Shore, C, 1993, 'Community' in Outhwaite W and Bottommore T, eds, *Blackwell Dictionary of Twentieth Century thought*, Blackwell, Oxford.
37. Chartered Institute of Housing, *NHF Standing Conference*, 13 October 1998, briefing paper by David Fotheringham.
38. London Pride Partnership, 1998 (note 16), 32.
39. Putnam R, 1993, *Making Democracy Work*, Princeton University Press, Princeton.
40. Fukuyama F, 1995, *Trust: Prosperity and the social virtues*, Penguin, Harmondsworth.
41. Page D and Boughton R, 1997 *Mixed Tenure Housing Estates: A study undertaken for Notting Hill*, Notting Hill Housing Association, London.
42. Ibid, 69.
43. Atkinson R and Kintrea K, 1998, *Reconnecting Excluded Communities: The neighbourhood impacts of owner occupation*, Scottish Homes, Edinburgh.
44. Cole I et al, 1997, *Creating Communities or Welfare Housing: A study of new housing association developments in Yorkshire/Humberside*, Chartered Institute of Housing, Coventry.
45. Ibid, 38.
46. Cole I and Shayer S, 1998, *Beyond Housing Investment: Regeneration, sustainability and the role of housing associations*, Centre for Regional Economic and Social Research, Sheffield Hallam University.
47. Used non-parametric Pearson Correlation.
48. Mean incomes of residents on tenure groups were estimated from the income questions on the survey and inequality measured as the difference in the means between each tenure group. If shared owners were also present, we considered the average income differences between all three tenure groups. That is always equivalent to two-thirds of the difference between the sole owners and social tenants, because shared owners always lie in between the two.
49. Evans R, 1998, *Housing Plus and Urban Regeneration: What works, why and where?*, The European Institute for Urban Affairs, Liverpool John Moores University, Liverpool, vii.
50. Miller D, [forthcoming], *The Dialectics of Shopping*, University of Chicago Press.
51. These findings should be treated with some caution because they reflect the experiences of those who were in when the interviewer called. These may not be a completely representative sample of the different demographic groups.
52. Forrest R and Kearns A, 1999, *Joined Up Places: Social cohesion and neighbourhood regeneration*, York Publishing Services, York.
53. Wellman B, 1998, 'The Network Community: An introduction to networks in the global village', in Wellman B, ed, *Networks in the Global Village*, Westview Press, Boulder Colorado.
54. Bridges G, 1994, *Gentrification, Class and Residence: A reappraisal*, Working

paper 109, SAUS, University of Bristol, 24.
55. Cole I et al, 1997 (note 44). Found that residents rated the mixed tenure development (Gordon Road) highest in overall satisfaction (86 per cent satisfied or very satisfied). Page and Boughton, 1997 (note 41), found satisfaction with area generally higher than national average on the four estates in west London which he considered, but some issues were rated below average.
56. Burrows R and Rhodes D, 1998, *Unpopular Places*, Policy Press, Bristol.
57. Of the 10 per cent of our entire sample who expressed their feeling for the estate as a whole by agreeing with the statements 'I don't like it very much' or 'I can't stand it', four per cent said that they thought mixing had brought problems, five per cent said that had not caused problems and one per cent did not have an opinion over whether it had caused problems or not.
58. Page and Boughton, 1997 (note 41).
59. Correlation coefficient of 0.22 with our broad ranking of levels of segregation.
60. Etzioni A, 1995 (note 4).
61. For example, Notting Hill Housing Association and the Housing Corporation are currently funding research by David Page into the economic impact of mixed tenure developments.
62. Mumford L, 1961, *The City in History*, Penguin, London, 572.
63. Wellman B, 1996 'Are personal communities local? A dumptarian reconsideration', *Social Networks*, no 18, 347-354.
64. Evans, 199 (note 49), 34.
65. Evans, 1998 (note 49).
66. Cl. Carole Roberts, quoted in *Fry's Hill: The new development fact sheet*, Oxford City Council.
67. Tyne and Wear Development Corporation, 1998, *The Power of a Decade of Achievement*, T&WDC, Newcastle, 11.
68. *SLFHA Annual Report 1997*, South London Family Housing Association, London.